PLAYLAND
and A PLACE
WITH THE
PIGS

BOOKS BY ATHOL FUGARD
AVAILABLE FROM TCG

Blood Knot & Other Plays
A Lesson from Aloes
Marigolds in August and The Guest
My Children! My Africa!
Notebooks: 1960–1977
The Road to Mecca
Statements

PLAYLAND
and A PLACE WITH THE PIGS

two plays by

ATHOL FUGARD

THEATRE COMMUNICATIONS GROUP
1993

Cover: Ben Halley, Jr. *(left)* as Martinus Zoeloe with Larry Golden as Gideon le Roux in the La Jolla Playhouse/Alliance Theatre Company co-production of *Playland*. Photograph copyright © 1993 by T. Charles Erickson.

Fugard, Athol.
[Playland]
Playland; and, A place with the pigs: two plays / Athol Fugard.
— 1st ed.
ISBN 1-55936-070-4 — ISBN 1-55936-071-2 (pbk.)
1. South Africa—Drama. I. Fugard, Athol. Place with the pigs.
1993.   II. Title.   III. Title: Place with the pigs.
PR9369.3.F8P59   1993   93-11834
822—dc20   CIP

Design and composition by The Typeworks
First Edition, November 1993

CONTENTS

PLAYLAND

For Yvonne Bryceland

Playland was first presented in the United States as a co-production of La Jolla Playhouse (Des McAnuff, Artistic Director, Terrence Dwyer, Managing Director) and Alliance Theatre Company (Kenny Leon, Artistic Director, Edith H. Love, Managing Director). The production, under the direction of the playwright, began performances in San Diego, California on August 25, 1992 and in Atlanta, Georgia on October 14, 1992. Set and costume design was by Susan Hilferty, lighting design by Dennis Parichy and sound design by David Budries. The cast was as follows:

Martinus Zoeloe	*Ben Halley, Jr.*
Gideon le Roux	*Larry Golden*
The voice of "Barking Barney" Barkhuizen	*Bill Flynn*

The play was originally produced by Mannie Manim at the Market Theatre, Johannesburg, South Africa on July 16, 1992.

NOTE

The South African Border War (1966–1989) was fought between
the South African Defense Force and the South West African
Police Force on one side and the South West African People's
Organization (SWAPO), supported by Cuban troops and
Russian armaments on the other. At stake was the territory of
South West Africa—now independent Namibia—which the
League of Nations had mandated to South Africa for supervision
after the First World War. The Border War was a long and bitter
struggle with heavy losses on both sides. Because of its traumatic
effect on the South African psyche, it is referred to as South
Africa's Vietnam. In addition, it was also a guerrilla war fought
in the bush and arid desert regions of the South West African/
Angolan border. The war ended in 1989 when a United Nations-
supervised truce and free elections led to the full independence
of the country. The majority party in the present government of
Namibia is the South West African People's Organization.

A glossary of some of the Afrikaans and English terms used
in *Playland* immediately follows the text.

SCENE 1

A small traveling amusement park encamped on the outskirts of a Karoo town. A large sign with the name PLAYLAND is prominently positioned. There is also an array of other gaudy signs advertising the various sideshows and rides—the Big Wheel, the Wall of Death, the Ghost Train and so on. They are all festooned with colored lights which will be switched on when the night gets under way. Battered speakers of a PA system at the top of a pole.

Foreground: the night watchman's camp: a broken car from one of the rides with a square of canvas stretched over it to provide shelter from sun and rain, and a paraffin tin brazier.

Time: the late afternoon of New Year's Eve, 1989.

Gideon le Roux saunters on. Casually but neatly dressed for a warm Karoo evening. He is stopped by the sound of an angry voice with laughter and heckling from other voices. Martinus Zoeloe walks on from the opposite side. Old overalls and a rolled-up balaclava on his head.

MARTINUS: Ja! Ja! Go on. Laugh as much as you like but I say it again: I'll see all of you down there in Hell. That's right. All of you. In Hell! And when you wake up and see the big fires and you start crying and saying you sorry and asking forgiveness, then it's me who is laughing.

Gideon stands quietly smoking a cigarette and listening to the harangue. Martinus is not aware of his presence.

Ja! That day it is Martinus who has a good laugh. You tell lies and cheat and drink and make trouble with the little girls and you think God doesn't know? He knows! He sees everything you do and when the Big Day of Judging comes he will say to you, and you, and specially you: Hey! You fucked the little girls in Cradock and gave them babies; you fucked the little girls in Noupoort and gave them babies—what you got to say for yourself? And you got nothing to say because it's true and that's the end of it. And all the times you verneuk the baas with the tickets and put the money in your pockets, He knows about that as well. And also the generator petrol you are stealing and selling in the location. Baas Barney swear at me, but I know it's you. I see you there by the petrol drums when you think nobody is looking. So voetsek to all of you! *(He sees the white man for the first time)*

GIDEON *(Applauding)*: That's it my friend. That's what I like to hear. Somebody who is not afraid to speak his mind. So you tell them. You tell them loud and clear.

MARTINUS: Joburg skollies. All of them. All they know is to make trouble for other people.

GIDEON: Then go make some for them. Ja. Report them to your baas. Don't let them get away with it. You got to speak up in this bloody world. It's the only way to put an end to all the nonsense that is going on. Everywhere you look—bloody nonsense! People think they can get away with anything these days. There's no respect left for nothing no more.

MARTINUS: That one with the skeel oog, he's the one. The first time I see him there in Beaufort West, when he comes looking for work, I knew! Skelm! And I warn Baas Barney. That one is trouble I tell him. But he wouldn't listen. So now we have it.

6

GIDEON: Then to hell with your Baas Barney as well! That's what I say. If he won't listen then too bad. You tried your best. My advice to you is just carry on and do your job and to hell with everything else. What is your job here?

MARTINUS: Watchman and handyman.

GIDEON: Night watchman for Playland. That sounds okay.

MARTINUS: Night and day watchman.

GIDEON: All the time?

MARTINUS: All the time. I watch everything all the time.

GIDEON: So when do you sleep?

MARTINUS: I don't sleep.

A silence settles between the two men. Gideon tries again.

GIDEON: Bloody hot again today, hey? On the news they said it was thirty-six degrees in the shade here by us. In the shade mark you! *(Hollow laugh)* I like that. I felt like phoning them and asking, is that now supposed to be a joke or what? Over by De Aar it was forty-one. Can you imagine? Chickens was dying of heatstroke. De Aar! *(Shakes his head)* God knows this dump is bad enough, but De Aar! No man, that's a fate worse than death. They say there's a ou bollie there who fries his breakfast eggs on his motorcar bonnet in summer. Says he uses multigrade instead of margarine. *(Hollow laugh. No response from Martinus)* Anyway that's how bad it is. Couple of months ago they offered me a transfer there with a pay rise. I turned it down flat. *(Pause)* By the way, what's your name?

MARTINUS: Martinus.

GIDEON: Martinus. That's a good one.

MARTINUS: Martinus Zoeloe.

GIDEON: That's sommer a bakgat name man! Martinus Zoeloe. BG. Buitengewoon. So listen Martinus, when do things get going around here? You know, the lights and the music and everything. When do you people switch on?

MARTINUS: Seven o'clock.

7

GIDEON *(Looking at his watch)*: Hour to go, then five more and it's hip-hip-hooray time hey! Goodbye 1989, welcome 1990! And 'bout bloody time too. Hell, this year now really went slowly hey? I thought we'd never get here. Some days at work it was so bad I use to think my watch had stopped. I check the time and I see it's ten o'clock. Two hours later I check it again and it's only half past ten. *(Hollow laugh. Nothing from Martinus)*

Didn't look as if it was going to be so bad in the beginning. I got my discharge at the end of February and it looked as if things were going to be okay—you know, being home, being alive . . . *(Hollow laugh)* and everything. I mean, shit man, there I was waking up in my own bed again with my old ma bringing me a cup of condensed-milk coffee the way I use to dream about it up there on the Border. Ja, March was also all right. I had some good times. Even April. But then. . . ! Shit-a-brick! June, July, August, September—fucking nothing man! All of them. Just nothing. And I tried. Believe me I tried, but I just couldn't get things going again. Every day I wake up and say to myself, "Come on now Gid, get your arse in gear and let's get things going today". . . but that's as far as it gets.

Like my pigeons. I use to be crazy about pigeons. Me and my dad. Just before he died we had over a hundred of them in a hok there in the backyard. Tumblers, pouters, homers, racers, fantails—we had them all. This was the time they use to flock—you know, all come together and fly around before settling into the hok for the night. Hell that was a beautiful sight man. Aerial maneuvers of the Karoo Squadron we use to call it. All the time in formation, round and round in the sky!

You would think they was following orders the way all of them would suddenly swerve and change direction . . . *(He laughs at the memory)*

Then after my dad died . . . I don't know . . . somehow

it just wasn't the same anymore without him. I kept them going and all that—fed them and cleaned the hok—but my heart wasn't in it the way it use to be when he was also there. Then one morning I go to feed them and—*Here!*—a wild cat or something had got into the hok in the night and gone mad! Half of them were lying around in pieces, man—dead as fucking freedom fighters. . . . I had to pull the necks of another ten of them that was still alive they was in such a bad way. That did it. I sold the rest of them and I thought that was the end of it. Not a damn! I'm sitting up there on the Border one day—and this is now years later, remember—and I suddenly find myself thinking about them and how lekker it would be to start up again—buy a few breeding pairs, fix up the hok and watch them fly at sunset. From then on that was all I use to think about. You got to have something to think about up there man, otherwise you go mad. I'm not joking. I've seen it happen. Anyway, the truth of the matter is I haven't done a bloody thing about it since I've been back. The old hok is still standing there on three legs, ready to fall over, full of spider webs. I don't know what it is man, but I just can't get things going again. I'm not bosbefok or anything like that. The doctors have given me some pills for my nerves and to help me sleep, but otherwise I'm okay. Ai! It's just. . . . I don't know. Like tonight. I was ready to just sit at home with my ma and fall asleep in front of the television again. Can you believe it? New Year's Eve? That's when I thought to myself, "No man, this has now gone far enough. Get out Gideon le Roux. Get among the people. Join in. Grab some fun. Look for romance!" So here I am ladies! Don't all rush at once. *(Hollow laugh)*

Anyway . . . that is going to be my resolution tonight when midnight comes: No bloody miseries next year! I don't care how I do it, but 1990 is going to be different. Even if it kills me, I'm going to get things going again.

You got yours ready?

MARTINUS: What?

GIDEON: Your New Year's resolution.

MARTINUS: What is that?

GIDEON: Midnight, man. When 1990 comes. You give up smoking or something like that.

MARTINUS: I don't smoke.

GIDEON: Then something else. Drinking.

MARTINUS: I don't drink.

GIDEON: Well there must be something you want to give up.

MARTINUS: No.

GIDEON: Okay. So you're perfect. Good luck to you. *(A hip flask of brandy appears out of a pocket)* That means I don't have to offer you a dop hey! *(Hollow laugh)*

Last year I gave up drinking. It lasted about ten minutes because then I needed a drink to give up smoking, and then I needed a drink *and* a cigarette to give up wanking— and that's not the capital of China my friend! And so it went. Every dop was another resolution . . . that lasted ten minutes! Base Camp Oshakati! That was quite a party. Talk about your friends going to Hell—if you had seen me and my buddies that night you would have sent the lot of us there as well.

Another silence. Both men stare at the horizon where a Karoo sunset is flaring to a dramatic climax.

How about that, hey!

MARTINUS: Ja, it's starting now.

GIDEON: It might have been a useless bloody year, but it's certainly going out in style. I mean, look at it! It's right around us. That's sommer a cinerama sunset for you.

MARTINUS: Ja, it's going to be a big one tonight.

GIDEON: We use to get them like that up in South West. From one end of the sky to the other—red, red. I'm telling you man, it looked like the end of the world had come. And believe me there was a couple of times when it also felt like that.

MARTINUS: The Day of Judgment.

GIDEON: That's a good one. I like it. Days of Judgment! Ja, for a lot of men that's what they turned out to be. And they were good men. My buddies! But that's the way it was. One day you're swapping jokes with him, the next day you're saying prayers for him . . . and wondering if it's your turn next. *(Pause)*

I can remember sitting there in the bush one day. It was about this time—late, late afternoon, nearly getting dark. That sky wasn't just red my friend, it was on fire! And you could smell it too. Smoke, burning rubber, ammo, dust, bush . . . everything! We'd had a big contact with SWAPO that day, and we weren't expecting it. They caught us napping. Jesus it was rough. Anyway, it was klaarstaan time again—sunset, sunrise, SWAPO's favorite times for a hit— and one of my buddies comes and parks next to me there in the trench. I say to him, "We're alive, Charlie. We're alive." And Charlie says, "You know Gid, I'm not so sure anymore that that's the good news." I always remember that. Because he was right. It always only got worse.

MARTINUS *(Gesturing at the sunset)*: I watch it every night. Every time it is different and I see different things.

GIDEON: Free bioscope!

MARTINUS: Last night it was like gold.

GIDEON: I didn't see it last night.

MARTINUS *(Pointing)*: That way, on the road to Beaufort West. Big, big piles of the gold that makes them all mad in Johannesburg. Mountains of gold!

GIDEON: How about that hey? Mountains of gold! We'd all be millionaires.

MARTINUS: And then sometimes nothing happens. The sun goes down slowly, slowly, and then it's gone. And then the

light goes away slowly, slowly, and then it's also gone, and
it's dark and the stars are shining.

GIDEON: They say it's just the dust in the atmosphere what does
it. You know . . . the colors and the clouds and everything.
But even so it still makes you think, doesn't it? Like over
there, that big one. Doesn't it look like they finally dropped
the atomic bomb on De Aar? I mean look at it. That's the
atomic-bomb cloud. What do they call it again? Ja, the
mushroom cloud!

MARTINUS: Tonight I see the fires of Eternal Damnation.

GIDEON: Hell, that's a heavy one.

MARTINUS: That's right, Hell!

GIDEON: Well, I suppose if you believe in that Bible stuff it
could be, but speaking for myself . . . *(Shakes his head)* no
thank you. I had the Bible shoved down my throat since I
was small and I'm gat-full of it now man. I've got a bad
dose of religious indigestion.

MARTINUS: Hell Fires on the Day of Judgment!

GIDEON: Don't get yourself all excited my friend, I've told you,
it's just dust in the atmosphere what does it. What they call
an optical illusion.

MARTINUS *(Laughs)*: It's coming!

GIDEON: What?

MARTINUS: The Day of Judgment. For everybody.

GIDEON: You've been listening to the dominees, haven't you?

MARTINUS: And when that day comes, everybody will stand
there and one by one *He* will call our names.

GIDEON: Ja, ja, I know. Time to meet your Maker and all the
rest of it. And for the sinners it's down to the old devil and
his braaivleis, and for the others it's up to the singing angels
for a happy ending. I don't want to spoil it for you
Martinus, but it happens to be fairy stories my friend,
stupid fairy stories, and I've heard them all. If you want to
believe them, that's your business. I don't. So if you don't
mind, keep them to yourself please. This is supposed to be

Playland, not Sunday School. I came here to have a little bit of fun, so let's keep it that way. Okay?

Another laugh from Martinus.

MARTINUS: Ja, that's the way it is. Playland is Happyland! Pretty lights and music. Buy your ticket for the Big Wheel and go round and round and forget all your troubles, all your worries.

    That's why they all come. I know. I watch them. Fifteen years I've been with Playland now, and all that time I am watching the people. Noupoort, Cradock, Hanover, Beaufort West, Laingsburg, Colesberg, Middelburg . . . all the places here in the Great Karoo. They pray for rain but they wait for Playland and the happiness machines. And when we switch on the lights and the music, they come. Like moths they come out of the night—the old uncles with the fat aunties, the young boys and the pretty girls, even the little children. They all come to play because they all want to forget.

    But it's no good. You can try to forget as hard as you like but it won't help, because all the things you did are written down in the Big Book, and when the day comes you will stand there and *He* will read them to you. And then what you got to say?

GIDEON: Plenty, my friend.

MARTINUS: Ja?

GIDEON: Oh ja! To start with, the so-called "Big Book." Just stop now for a moment and try to imagine just how big that book has got to be if what everybody is doing wrong down here is written in it. Ja. You ever thought about that? There's a lot of people in this world, Mr. Martinus Zoeloe, and a hell of a lot of "doing wrong" going on all the time. And also who the hell is writing it all down? They'll need more than shorthand up there if they want to keep up with what's going on down here, that I can tell you.

Martinus holds up the five fingers of one hand and the thumb of the other.

What is that?

MARTINUS *(Unperturbed)*: Number Six is the big one.

GIDEON: Number Six what?

MARTINUS: The Ten Commandments. Number Six, "Thou shalt not kill." That's the big one. Not even your enemy. Not even the man you hate more than anything in the world. If you steal something you can always give it back. If you tell a lie, you can always still tell the truth. But when you kill a man you take his life and you can't give that back. He's dead, and that's the end of it.

GIDEON *(Agitated)*: So why you telling me all this?

MARTINUS: It's in the Bible.

GIDEON *(Sharply)*: I know it's in the Bible. What I'm asking is why you telling me. You think I'm stupid or something? I learnt all about the commandments in Sunday School thank you very much. So just keep your sermons to yourself, okay? If you want to play dominee go preach to those skollie friends of yours.

And anyway, everybody knows there's times when you got to do it.

MARTINUS: What?

GIDEON: Number Six.

MARTINUS: No.

GIDEON: Yes there is! What about self-defense?

Martinus shakes his head.

Or protecting women and children?

Martinus shakes his head again.

What about Defending Your Country Against
Communism?

MARTINUS *(Doggedly)*: Aikona!

GIDEON *(Beside himself with frustration)*: Those are all times
when it's all right to do it! Even the bloody dominees say
so. I've heard them myself. Sermons up in the Operational
Area.

MARTINUS *(Implacable)*: No. The Bible says "Thou shalt not
kill thy neighbor."

GIDEON: So who the hell is talking about neighbors? I'm talking
about criminals and communists! No man, this little
discussion of ours is now getting out of hand.

(Restraining himself) Listen Martinus, I don't want to
start a bad argument between us so let me tell you again,
and this is now really for the last time, okay? I am gat-full
of the Bible. I don't need another dose of it. Do I make
myself clear?

You've now really got it on the brain, haven't you? Don't
you ever talk about anything else?

MARTINUS: Like what?

GIDEON: Like anything, for God's sake. Rugby. Women. Even
bloody politics would be better. Talk ANC if you like—all
that one-man-one-vote kak—but just change the record for
God's sake!

(Another drink) Somebody I would have liked you to
meet is Ou Tollie—he was the bushman tracker with our
unit. He knew what the score was. Never use to join us for
church services—just sit there on one side under a
thornbush and watch us singing our hymns, saying our
prayers, and the dominees sermonizing about Heaven and
Hell and all the rest of it. So one day I asked him what he
thought about things. You know what he said? "When we
die, we die. The wind blows away our footprints and that is
the end of us." Ou Tollie! Ja, he knew what the score was.

They been up there you know. Right round the earth, to

the moon and back . . . they even getting ready now to go to Mars . . . and what's more they also got pictures of everything up there, and guess what, my friend . . . there's no sign of your Heaven and Hell anywhere! Put that in your old Bantu pipe and smoke it. Ja! Science my friend, science! There's a thing up there called a satellite that is going all the way to the End of the World and it's taking pictures all the time and sending them back and all you can see is outer space . . . miles and miles of bugger-all. It's almost as bad as the Karoo up there. So I don't know where you think your angels are flying around, but it's certainly nowhere up in the big blue sky, that I can tell you.

Martinus listens calmly.

And finally my friend, just in case you haven't noticed, I would like to point out that the Fires of Eternal Damnation have now gone out, so where the hell is the party?

Martinus stares at him blankly.

It's quarter past seven man. Nearly twenty past.
MARTINUS: So?
GIDEON: So, where's the lights and music? You told me things get going at seven o'clock.
MARTINUS: That's right.
GIDEON: Well for God's sake I'm telling you it's past seven o'clock. *(He shows his watch)* Look for yourself if you don't believe me.

Martinus shrugs his shoulders indifferently.

Now what the hell is that supposed to mean?
MARTINUS: Maybe the generators is broken down again.

There's lots of trouble with the generators. Last month in Noupoort, two nights the generators broke down.

GIDEON: So what must we do?

MARTINUS: Wait. They will try to fix it.

GIDEON (*Huge disbelief*): I don't believe it! We get ourselves all nicely dressed up, drive for bloody miles to get here, and now we must just stand around and wait like a lot of bloody sheep while they *try* to fix the generators. How long does it take them?

MARTINUS: Sometimes they fix it quick. Sometimes it takes a long time. Sometimes they can't fix it and must send away for spare parts.

GIDEON: And then?

MARTINUS: Nothing.

GIDEON: Nothing what?

MARTINUS: Then nothing happens tonight. Everybody must go home. Last month in Noupoort . . .

GIDEON: To hell with what happened last month in Noupoort. I'm not remotely interested in Noupoort's troubles. They can drop an atomic bomb on that dump as well as far as I'm concerned.

Pause. Martinus calm, Gideon agitated.

No man. This is about as much nonsense as a man can take. What a bloody year. No doubt about it now . . . the worst one of my entire life. With all my will power I hang on until we get to the last arsehole day of it, then I make a special effort and pull myself together and get out of the house, and where do I land up?

A broken-down Playland! And now you tell me I must just go back home if they can't fix the generator? No, my friend. Oh no! You can maybe sell that bullshit to those railway japies in Noupoort, but nobody is going to buy it over here. We weren't born yesterday. If you want to call yourselves Playland you better prove it tonight, otherwise good old Baas Barney will start the New Year with more than just his generators broken.

The PA system suddenly crackles into life with static and feedback whine.

BARNEY *(A voice over the PA system)*: Testing, testing, one, two, three, four, testing. Can you hear me Martinus?
MARTINUS *(Shouting back)*: I can hear you Baas Barney!
BARNEY: Loud and clear?
MARTINUS: Loud and clear Baas Barney.
BARNEY: All right Jackson—switch on.

The lights of Playland start flickering and after a few false starts they come on and stay on.

MARTINUS *(A good laugh at Gideon)*: There. . . . Look! Listen! Pretty lights and music! Go forget your troubles white man. Playland is open and waiting for you.

Gideon leaves.

SCENE 2

Gideon in the bright lights and loud music of Playland.

BARNEY *(On the PA)*: Hello everybody, hello and hello again. Welcome to Playland. This is your Master of Ceremonies, your old friend "Barking Barney" Barkhuizen promising you a sensational, a spectacular evening of fun and thrills to end the year. We've got a wonderful program lined up and to start the ball rolling, here is a special New Year's Eve offer: Buy nine tickets for any of the rides and you get one free—and remember, hang on to your ticket stubs because you could be the winner of one of our fabulous prizes. There's a draw every hour on the hour! So what are you waiting for? Let's rock out the old and roll in the new. . . . One, two, three and away we go. . . !

An energetic piece of rock-and-roll sets the tone and tempo of the evening. Playland is now in full swing. From the speakers at the top of the pole a pastiche of old pop songs, rock-and-roll and Boeremusiek. Interspersed with these is Barney's voice making announcements about the various sideshows and rides, lucky ticket numbers, lost children and so on and, continuously, the squeaks and shrieks of laughter and terror from people on the rides.

(Interrupting a pop song) Hold everything everybody. Your attention please. This is a very special announcement. She is blonde, she is beautiful, she is Marie du Toit and she is eighteen years old today. So come on everybody . . . *(Singing)* "Happy birthday to you . . ." *(And so on)*

More pop music.

Your attention please. Your attention. Please check your ticket stubs because if you are the holder of number eight-zero-four-six, I repeat . . . eight-zero-four-six . . . you have just won yourself and your partner the famous gut-buster platter at the Happy Rustler Steakhouse. Come to the information desk for your voucher. Our next draw will be for a fashion perm at Maison Capri, so hurry up and buy your tickets for the Big Wheel, the Whip . . .

More pop music.

This is the lost-property department speaking . . . will the

parents of little Willie Liebenberg please come to the
caravan next to the Wall of Death . . . the parents of little
Willie Liebenberg please . . .

More pop music.

Your attention please, your attention! This is an emergency
announcement. Will anyone with an empty and rumbling
stomach please report immediately to the stall next to the
Rifle Range. We have a sizzling stack of our famous Karoo
burgers and Boere dogs in need of urgent gastromedi-
nomical attention. I repeat, anyone . . .

*More pop music. Gideon is in the middle of all this, trying too
hard to have a good time. He tells jokes, tries to sing along
with the music, and wisecracks about the PA announcements,
creating an image of forced and discordant gaiety.*

SCENE 3

*Later. The night watchman's camp. Martinus alone. Gideon
returns. Brandy and desperation give a new, aggressive edge to
his behavior. He wears a silly paper hat and carries a
noisemaker.*

GIDEON *(Singing)*:
". . . baby don't you know I love you so
Can't you feel it when we touch
I will never never let you go
I love you Oh so much."
. . . but I don't mean you poephol! *(Hollow laugh)*
How you doing there Marty?
MARTINUS: You back.

GIDEON: Ja me. Who else? Your old friend Corporal Gideon le
    Roux.

MARTINUS: Corporal?

GIDEON: That's it. Two stripes. But listen, forget about the
    rank. Just call me Gid. I been thinking about it you see and
    what do you say we must just let bygones be bygones? I
    want us to be buddies. Me and you. Gid and Marty. Okay?

MARTINUS: Okay.

GIDEON *(Holding out his hand)*: Put it there.

They shake.

So then tell me, how is things with you Marty?

MARTINUS *(Humoring him)*: I'm doing all right Gid.

GIDEON: Then why you looking so sad man? I'm sitting up
    there on top of the Big Wheel, admiring the view, looking
    down and seeing everything and everybody and there, in
    the corner, all by his lonely self, I see my buddy, poor old
    Marty. Everybody else was having such a good time but
    you were just sitting there looking so sad. Cheer up man!
    It's not the end of the world yet, just the end of a totally
    useless bloody year—and we're nearly there Marty! Two
    more hours to go and then it's Happy New Year!

MARTINUS: You having a good time hey Gid?

GIDEON: You bet. I'm having myself one hell of a good time.
    I've tried everything out there—the Lucky Fishpond,
    shooting wooden ducks with a pellet gun, ping-pong balls
    in the clown's mouth . . . you name it, I've done it. And all
    the rides as well. Just between you and me, the Ghost Train
    is now really bloody stupid—kid's stuff you know. . . . But
    the Big Wheel. . . ! Three times man. Round and round
    and up and down. Whoopee! And you know something, it
    is just like you said—I've forgotten all my troubles. How
    about that! My sick ma, my stupid job, the stupid bloody

foreman at my stupid bloody job, my stupid bloody car
that I already know won't start when I want to go home—
you've got to give me a push, okay?—I've forgotten them
all! And I'm not finished. I'm going back for more. I want
to go round and round and up and down until I even
forget who the bloody hell I am!

(Hollow laugh) How's that?

MARTINUS: That's very good Gid. But then why you here?

GIDEON: Why am I here? That's a very good question.

MARTINUS: The Big Wheel is over there. There's nothing for
you here.

GIDEON: Oh yes there is! You! My buddy. You are here so that's
why I am here. First thing you learn up there in the bush.
Don't ever desert a buddy.

MARTINUS: You won't forget your troubles if you sit here with me.

GIDEON: Hey hey hey! Marty. Why you talking like that man?
If I didn't know you so well I would say you was trying to
get rid of me. You're not trying to do that are you . . .
because if you were, then you hurt my feelings man. Eina!
You hurt my feelings bad! (Hollow laugh)

It's only a joke. Hell Marty, listen, as one buddy to
another let me give you a gentle word of advice. Lighten up
a little bit man. You know, try a little smile or a chuckle
now and then. It can be very heavy going with you
sometimes.

Anyway, jokes aside now, if you want to know the truth,
the whole truth and nothing but the truth so help me God,
I came back here because I got something for you. A
present. Ja. I mean it when I say I was thinking about you
out there. You ask the others that were up there on the
Border with me—Ou Charlie, or Stan, or Neelsie—all of
them. They'll tell you Corporal Gideon le Roux was always
thinking of his buddies. Because that is the way I was
brought up—to think about others.

So I've got a wonderful present for you. It's going to

make you very happy. It's better than a hundred rides on the Big Wheel because it won't just help you forget your troubles, it's going to get rid of them for you . . . and for keeps, my buddy. That's a money-back guarantee. You ready for it? It's a New Year's resolution that I made up specially for you to deal with all your problems. When midnight comes, you must stand to attention . . . *(He gets Martinus standing to attention, removes his balaclava and puts his paper hat on Martinus's head)* raise your right hand and say, "I, Martinus Zoeloe, do solemnly swear that my New Year's resolution for 1990 is . . . No More Dominees! No More Sermons from the Dominees! No More Bible Stories from the Dominees! No More Bullshit from the Dominees! Hallelujah and Amen!"

(A big hollow laugh) How's that Marty. I'm telling you man, that is the answer to all your problems, because that is where they come from—those black crows up there in the pulpit taking advantage of simple-minded people like you. You make that your resolution tonight and I promise you my friend that in 1990 you will be a happy man.

MARTINUS: Like you.

GIDEON: Ja, like me. Well? I'm waiting Marty.

Martinus studies Gideon in silence for a few seconds then goes up to him and puts the paper hat back on his head. He retrieves his balaclava and returns to his seat.

Is it my imagination Marty, or do you now not really care too much for my present? Hey? I know you are not the excitable sort but even so, can't you try to squeeze out a little "Thank you, Gid"? Haai Marty, I can see you want to break my heart tonight. Why my buddy? What have I done? That heart is full of good feelings for you. Don't hurt it. That's not the way buddies treat each other.

MARTINUS: You make jokes about your heart, but you must be

careful with it. Because *He* can see into it.

GIDEON: Who? Chris Barnard? *(Laughs)* Joke Marty! Joke.

MARTINUS: All the secrets you hide away there—the big ones, the bad ones—it's no good because *He* knows them.

GIDEON Marty . . . I've got a horrible feeling you are starting again.

MARTINUS: He knows them all. Ja! Like a skelm in the night looking for your money under your mattress. *He* comes when you are sleeping and *He* finds them and looks at them.

GIDEON: Ja! There you go again—more bloody dominee talk.

MARTINUS: It's not dominee talk.

GIDEON: Yes it is. I know the sound of dominee talk like I use to know the sound of a good cabbage fart from my dad.

MARTINUS: *He* told me so himself.

GIDEON: Who?

MARTINUS: *Him.*

GIDEON: Him?

MARTINUS: Ja.

GIDEON: Oh I see. This is now the Big Baas himself we're talking about.

Martinus nods.

He spoke to you.

MARTINUS: Ja.

GIDEON: God.

MARTINUS: God Almighty.

GIDEON: He came around here and had a little chat with you.

MARTINUS: It was in a dream. He talked to me in a dream.

For a few seconds Gideon is speechless.

GIDEON *(Defeated)*: No. No! That's it. I give up. I surrender. I'm waving the white flag Marty.

MARTINUS *(Imperturbable as ever)*: I dreamed that I was
  praying like the dominee said I must. I was kneeling and
  telling *Him* that I was sorry for what I did and wanted
  forgiveness. And then I heard Him. "It's no good Martinus.
  I can see into your heart. I can see you are not sorry for
  what you did." So I said "That's true God. I am not sorry."
  And He said "Then I can't forgive and you must go to Hell.
  All the people who are not sorry for what they did will go
  to Hell."

GIDEON: Just like that.

MARTINUS: Ja.

GIDEON: And then you woke up.

MARTINUS: Ja.

GIDEON: And you believed it.

MARTINUS: Ja.

GIDEON: And now you also want me to believe it.

MARTINUS: Ja.

GIDEON: Hell Marty, you're asking for a lot tonight. First it's the
  Bible stories I must believe and now it's your dreams. . . !

  (Beginning to lose patience again) What's the matter with
  you man? You can't believe them like they was real, like
  they was something that really happened to you. A dream
  . . . is just a bloody dream. It's what goes on in your head
  when you are sleeping, when your eyes are closed. Like
  when you imagine things. Don't you even know the
  difference between that and what is real? Must I also now
  explain that to you?

*Martinus says nothing. Gideon pursues the subject with
morbid persistence.*

Real is what you can believe because you can touch it, and
see it, and smell it . . . with your eyes wide open. Next time
you sit there in the bush and have a boskak, have a good
look at what you leave there on the ground, because that is

what real means. When you can show me Heaven and Hell like I can show you shit, then I'll listen to the dominees and believe all their Bible stories.

(Brandy bottle reappears) And let me just also say that for somebody who is so certain he is on his way to Hell, you seem to be taking things very easy buddy boy. According to your Bible that is a fairly serious state of affairs you know. It's not like going to jail. When you get down there, you stay down there. There's no such thing as getting time off for good behavior. It's a one-way ticket my friend. Suffering and agony nonstop. And forever. But if you got no problems with that, then okay. Good luck to you. *(Takes a swig from his bottle)*

What did you do Marty? What's the charge the Big Baas is going to read out of the Big Book when the Big Day comes? Must have been a good one if he's given you a one-way ticket for it. Come on man you can tell me. I know how to keep a secret. We're buddies now, remember. Buddies always share their secrets Marty.

Still no response from Martinus.

(Continues in a conspiratorial whisper) It was Number Six wasn't it? The Big One. You killed somebody hey. That's why the Big Baas is so the hell in with you.

(Elated laughter) Ja, I knew it man. I'm telling you, the moment I saw you I smelt it. I said to myself "Be careful Gid. There's something about that bugger."

MARTINUS: Go back to Playland Gid. Go ride the Big Wheel.

GIDEON *(More laughter. He continues greedily)*: Not a damn. I'm having a good time here with you. So come on man. Spill the beans. What happened? Housebreaking and theft? Armed robbery? No. You don't look like that sort. You're not one of those skollies. Something else . . . wait a bit, wait a bit, I've got it! Your woman. Right? You caught your woman with another man! How's that?

MARTINUS: Leave me alone.

GIDEON *(Laughter)*: Looks like I'm getting hot. Who got it
Marty? Your woman? The man? Both of them? *(Still more
laughter)* How did you do it? Knife? Did you get away
with it?

MARTINUS: I'm telling you again, leave me alone.

GIDEON: Come now Marty, don't take it personally. I'm only
trying to help. All I want is to help you deal with your
problems.

MARTINUS: You got no help for me. So go!

GIDEON *(Brutally)*: No!

MARTINUS: What do you want here?

GIDEON: The fucking truth. That's what I want. You killed
somebody. It's written all over you man. Think I'm blind?
And I want to know who it was.

MARTINUS: I'm telling you nothing.

GIDEON: Oh yes?

MARTINUS: Yes! Nothing!

Pause. Gideon backs out of the developing confrontation.

GIDEON: Okay, if that's the way you want it. I reckon that's the
end of buddies then.

MARTINUS: Yes! So go back to your own people.

GIDEON: What people? That fucking herd of Karoo zombies
out there grazing on candy floss? My people? Shit! Any
resemblance between me and them is purely coaccidental.
You try to talk to them, exchange a few friendly words and
they look at you as if you were a fucking freak or
something. Playland! Ja, that's where they belong. Two
rand to shoot wooden ducks with a pellet gun. We weren't
shooting wooden ducks with pellet guns up there on the
Border, my friend. While that crowd of fat arses were
having joyrides in Playland we were in Hell. Ja! For your

information you don't have to wait for Judgment Day to
find out what that word means. Hell is right here and now.
I can take you to it. It's called the Operational Area and it's
not everlasting bonfires either. It's everlasting mud and piss
and shit and sweat and dust. And if you want to see the
devil I can show you him as well. He wears a khaki
uniform, he's got an AK-47 in his hands.

MARTINUS: SWAPO.

GIDEON: Ja, that's his name. And he wasn't shooting at wooden
ducks either.

MARTINUS: Did you kill him?

GIDEON: The devil? *(Hollow laugh)* Ja, I killed him. How else
do you think I'm here? That's the only way you stayed
alive. The Law of the Jungle! That's what we use to say. Kill
or be killed . . . and don't think about it.

MARTINUS *(Pointing at Gideon and laughing triumphantly)*:
Number Six! You also. Number Six! I'll see you in Hell
Corporal Gideon le Roux.

GIDEON *(With all the vulgarity he can muster)*: Fuck you!

MARTINUS *(His laughter cut short)*: Hey!

GIDEON: That's right. I'll say it again. Fuck you! You can shove
Number Six right up your arse. And don't point your
fucking finger at me again. It's rude, my boy.

MARTINUS: Aikona!

GIDEON: Aikona yourself. I'm telling you to mind your own
business Martinus Zoeloe. The secrets in my heart have got
nothing to do with you or anybody else.

MARTINUS *(Restraining himself)*: Okay. I mind my own
business. And you also. The secrets in my heart got
nothing to do with you. So go. There is nothing for you
here. This is my place.

GIDEON: Your place?

MARTINUS: Ja. My place. This is the night watchman's place. I
am the night watchman. You go somewhere else.

GIDEON: Don't you tell me to go! This is still a free country.

You people haven't taken over yet. *(His brandy bottle is empty. He hurls it away and leaves)*

SCENE 4

Later. Gideon is back in the bright lights and loud music of Playland. He is a dark, brooding presence watching the world with smoldering resentment. Everybody is getting ready for the arrival of the New Year.

BARNEY *(On the PA, attempting an American accent)*: Good evening ladies and gentlemen and welcome to this Karoo Broadcasting Corporation New Year's Eve Special. I am your KBC host for the evening—"Barking Barney" Barkhuizen—speaking to you live from Cape Karooveral where the space shuttle Playland is waiting on the launching pad . . . primed and ready for her blastoff into 1990. According to the countdown clock there is now only three minutes left before ignition so get ready folks to wave 1989 goodbye. The weather forecast continues to be favorable—for the launch and for romance—starry skies and a balmy breeze. Mission control informs us that the countdown is proceeding smoothly so it looks as if we're all set for another successful launch at the stroke of midnight.

And now there is only two minutes to go. An expectant hush is settling over the large crowd gathered here to participate in this historic event. Looking at the closed-circuit television monitors I can see that all the gastronauts in Playland are putting away the last of their Karoo burgers and Boere dogs and are now buckling up and bracing themselves for the G-forces that are going to spin them off into Playland's 1990 Orbit of Happiness. One minute to go! We've still got the green light on all systems. The tension is unbearable ladies and gentlemen as the countdown clock ticks its way through the last seconds of 1989. On everybody's lips, the same whispered prayer, Thank God it's over. Twenty seconds left as we line up for the final countdown . . . and here it comes. . . !!

Ten-nine-eight-seven-six-five-four-three-two-one-ZERO!!!

We have a launch! We-have-a-launch! Yes, ladies and gentlemen, Playland has lifted off into 1990 . . .

The New Year arrives with an explosion of sound—voices singing, voices cheering, motor-car hooters, sirens, fireworks . . . a cacophony that imperceptibly begins to suggest the sound of battle. Gideon's contribution is to make as much "Happy New Year" noise as he can, ending up with the singing of "Auld Lang Syne." This gets progressively more violent and finally degenerates into a wild, wordless animal sound. When he stops, all is silent. He hears nothing except his breathing and his heart beating.

GIDEON: Easy Gid . . . you're alive! . . . easy does it . . . you're alive . . . it's over . . . it's all over and you're alive . . .

The sounds of Playland fade back in.

SCENE 5

Later. The night watchman's camp. Martinus is alone. Midnight has come and gone and all that is left of the celebrations is a few distant and receding sounds of revelry. The last piece of music—"Goodnight Sweetheart"—is playing over the PA system.

BARNEY *(Now a tired, off-duty voice)*: Okay everybody, that's it. Cash up and bring your ticket rolls and money to the caravan. Give it a few more seconds Jackson and then you can start to switch off. And Martinus, make sure everything is locked up properly tonight. We're too near that damned location for my liking. They've got to give us a better site next time otherwise we're not coming here again. New Year's Eve and we only had half the crowd we had at De Aar last month. This lot should go over there for a few lessons in how to have a good time. *Here*, it was hard going tonight. *(A long and audible yawn)* Ek is moeg, kêrels. Ek is moeg!

A few more seconds and then the music is cut off abruptly and Playland's illuminations start to go out. Gideon returns yet again to Martinus. He stands silently. Martinus is getting ready for his night shift—old overcoat and kierie.

MARTINUS: It's finished white man. It's all over for tonight. Time for you to go home now. You heard what the music said, "Goodnight Sweetheart, it's time to go."

(He laughs) Ja, everybody is sad when the happiness machine stop and the lights go out. But don't worry. You can come again tomorrow. Your Playland is safe. Martinus will watch it for you. Martinus will watch all your toys and tomorrow you can come and play again.

But now it is my time! Now night watchman Martinus Zoeloe is in charge.

Ja! You want to know about me white man. Okay. I tell you this. I know how to watch the night and wait for trouble. That is my job. While all the sweethearts are lying in bed with their sweet dreams, that is what I am doing—watching the night and waiting for trouble. I do it well. A long time ago I learnt how to sit with the ghosts and look and listen and wait—and that time I was waiting for big trouble white man . . . bigger trouble than a few drunk location skollies looking for mischief. So they can come and try their nonsense. I am ready for them!

He brandishes his kierie in traditional style and then sets out on his rounds. Gideon blocks his path.

GIDEON: Where you going?

MARTINUS: To do my job.

GIDEON: No.

MARTINUS: No what?

GIDEON: You're not going anywhere.

MARTINUS: Why not?

GIDEON: Because I say so, that's why. You stay right where you are. Don't think you can just switch off the fucking lights and tell me to go home, because I'm telling you it's not over.

MARTINUS: It is, white man. Look! There's nobody left. I tell you Playland is finished for tonight.

GIDEON: Fuck Playland! I'm talking about you and me. That's what it's all about now. You and me. Nice and simple. No complications. You and me. There's things to settle between us, and now is the time to do it. Right now . . . right here.

MARTINUS: There is nothing between you and me.

Gideon laughs.

What do you want from me white man? All night you keep coming back. For what? If you want to make trouble go do it with your own people.

GIDEON: Fuck them as well. I'm not interested in them. It's you I want. I want to make some nice trouble with you.

MARTINUS: Why? What did I do to you? Nothing!

GIDEON (*Another wild laugh*): Nothing?

MARTINUS: Yes! I sit here. I mind my own business and then you come. You come again and again. I didn't call you. I do nothing to you.

GIDEON: Nothing, Swapo?

MARTINUS: My name is not Swapo.

GIDEON: It is now. I'm calling you Swapo. If you're not my buddy, that's who you are.

MARTINUS: My name is Martinus Zoeloe.

GIDEON: Martinus Zoeloe se gat!! Name? What the fuck are you talking about? You haven't got a name. You're just a number. Number one, or number two, number three. . . . One day I counted you twenty-seven fucking times. I bury you every night in my sleep. You're driving me mad Swapo. And you call that nothing?

MARTINUS *(Disturbed by Gideon's violent ramblings)*: Haai, haai! You are mad. I'm not talking to you no more.

He makes another determined move to leave. Gideon blocks his path again.

GIDEON: I said no.

MARTINUS: Let me go.

GIDEON: No. I told you, you're not going anywhere. I haven't finished with you.

MARTINUS *(Rising anger)*: To hell with you. I've finished with you. Get out of my way.

GIDEON: Make me. Go ahead. Make me. *(He starts pushing Martinus back)*

MARTINUS: Don't do that.

GIDEON *(Another push)*: I'll do any fucking thing I like.

MARTINUS: I warn you white man.

GIDEON *(Another push)*: About what, black man? Warn me about what? You trying to scare me? Don't flatter yourself. There's fuck-all you can say or do that will scare me. But if you want to try something, go ahead.

The two men are on the brink of real physical violence.

So what are you waiting for? Come, let's see what you can do.

MARTINUS *(Breaking away)*: No Martinus! Stop! *(He makes a supreme effort to control himself. He returns and confronts Gideon)* Gideon le Roux! I say your name. Please now, listen to me. I put down my kierie. I tell you nicely, I don't want to make trouble with you. Don't you make trouble with me. Leave me alone. Because if we make trouble for each other tonight, then I know what happens.

GIDEON: Oh yes?

MARTINUS: Yes! I will do it again. S'true's God. I do it again.

GIDEON: What?

MARTINUS: Number Six.

GIDEON: Good old Number Six! So I was right. You did kill somebody.

MARTINUS: I killed a white man.

GIDEON: You bullshitting me? You still trying to scare me?

MARTINUS: Andries Jacobus de Lange, the Deceased. I killed him.

GIDEON: You're telling the truth. *(Laughter)* How about that! It gets better and better. In fact, it's fucking perfect. *(More laughter out of a violent, dark elation)*

I knew it. I knew it all along. The moment I saw you I knew there was something . . . you know . . . between us—me and you. And there it is. You killed a white man. Now we can get down to real business.

MARTINUS: No! There is nothing between you and me.

GIDEON *(Laughter)*: Oh yes there is.

(Singing)
"I will never, never let you go
I love you Oh so much!"

Who was he? The white man?

Nothing from Martinus.

Listen Swapo, there's a lot of shit we got to clean up

tonight, so you better start talking. What happened?

MARTINUS: My woman, she worked for him. For his wife and children. The housework and the washing.

GIDEON: You see! I knew it! I knew there was a woman in it.

MARTINUS: It was in Port Elizabeth. I had a job in the cement factory there. I was saving money to get married. Thandeka, my woman, was living at the white people's house. On Sundays she comes to visit me in the location. And so it was until one day when she comes to me I see that she is unhappy. I asked her what was wrong but she wouldn't tell me anything. Then another time when she comes she was crying and I asked her again and then she told me. She said the white man was coming all the time to her room in the backyard and trying to get into bed with her. She always said no to him and pushed him out. But then one night he beat her and forced her to get into the bed with him.

GIDEON: And then?

MARTINUS: I killed him.

GIDEON: How? How did you do it?

MARTINUS: A knife.

GIDEON: Ja! You bastards like the knife, don't you?

MARTINUS: I sent my woman away. I waited in her room. When the white man opened the door and came in I had my knife ready and I killed him.

GIDEON: Just like that.

MARTINUS: Just like that.

GIDEON: Did he fight?

MARTINUS: Yes, but he wasn't strong, so I killed him quickly. He's in Hell. He didn't even have time to pray to God.

GIDEON: Number Six!

MARTINUS: Number Six. And I'm *not* sorry. When the judge asked me if I was, I told him. I told him that if I saw that white man tomorrow I would kill him again. So then he sentenced me to death and my woman to fifteen years. He

wouldn't believe her when she told him what the white
man did to her. He said that we killed him because we
wanted to rob the house.

GIDEON: Why didn't they hang you?

MARTINUS: They nearly did. I sat in the death cell six months
waiting for the rope. I was ready for it. But when there was
just three days to go the white man's wife went to the judge
and told him that my woman was telling the truth. She
told him that her husband had forced other servants to get
into his bed. So then they changed my sentence to fifteen
years. They let my woman go free. I never saw her again.
That is my story.

GIDEON: Story my arse! It's a fucking joke man. A bad joke.
You killed that poor bugger just for that? Just for screwing
your woman? *(Laughter)*

  You people are too funny. Listen my friend, if screwing
your woman is such a big crime, then you and your
brothers are going to have to put your knives into one hell
of a lot of white men . . . starting with me! Ja. What's the
matter with you? Were you born yesterday? We've all done
it. And just like you said, knocked on that door in the
backyard, then drag her onto the bed and grind her arse off
on the old coir mattress. That's how little white boys learn
to do it. On your women!

  And you want to know something else, Swapo? They
like it from us! Your woman was crying crocodile tears. I
bet you anything you like she had a bloody good time there
with the baas humping away on top of her.

*Martinus rigid, every muscle tense as he tries to control the
impulse to throw himself at Gideon.*

Now do you understand what I'm saying? If you want to
kill that white man again, now's your chance. He's standing
right here in front of you.

(He waits) Come on! What you waiting for? Try to make it two. You got nothing to lose Swapo. You already got your one-way ticket. You can't go to Hell twice.

You think you're big stuff don't you because you killed one white man? That's your score. One! And now you think you can maybe make it two. One . . . two. *(Laughter)* What a bloody joke! You're an amateur, man. What you did was child's play. I was with the pros and for ten years we were up there on the Border sending your freedom-fighting brothers to Hell, and I'm not talking about one or two. We were into double figures, man. One amazing bloody day I did the rounds and counted twenty-seven of them that we'd blown away to Kingdom Come. Ja! Twenty-fucking-seven. Do you have the remotest idea what that means? What it feels like to count twenty-seven dead men? You had to have a strong stomach for it my friend. Those brothers of yours were full of shit, and I don't mean their politics. I mean the real stuff. They started stinking even before the sun had cooked them up a bit, because when that happened, when they'd been in the oven for a couple of days, as we use to say, then I'm telling you, you didn't eat meat for a week.

(Speaking with manic intensity) That was the first thing I use to do you see. When it was all over—the shooting and screaming—all that fucking noise like the world was coming to an end, when suddenly it was quiet like now, I would take a deep breath, say to myself "You're alive, Gid," then walk around and count. I always wanted to know how many there were, you see. Even before the OC asked for a body count I was out there doing it. You could take your time you see, walk around slowly and carefully and do it properly like my pa use to do when he counted his cabbages in the backyard. The Oubaas was crazy about cabbages man, specially the way my ma use to cook it for him, in a pot with nice pieces of fat mutton. It made him

fart like an Impala ready for takeoff, but he had to have his cabbage. So every morning it was "Come Gideon, let's go count our blessings," and I would hold his hand and walk next to him and say nicely after him "One cabbage, two cabbage, three cabbage . . ." that's how I learnt to count. Even before I was in school man I knew how to count my blessings. But now it wasn't cabbages anymore, it was "One Swapo, two Swapo, three Swapo. . . . " My very first time I counted there was eight of them. Shit man, that was something new for me. The only dead person I had ever seen was my pa when we all said goodbye to him in his coffin and now suddenly there I was counting eight of them—lying all over the place, some of them with pieces missing. Then for a long time it looked as if fifteen was going to be the record until that follow-up when we ambushed a whole bloody unit . . . and when it came time to count. . . ! Twenty-fucking-seven of them! I couldn't believe it man. A new record! "Twenty-seven Swapo cabbages in the garden daddy!"

He salutes. Martinus just stares at him.

So where's your sense of humor? That's a joke. Didn't you get it? Swapo cabbages. I counted the dead men like my pa use to count his fucking cabbages. So don't just stand there and stare at me like a bloody baboon. Laugh!

MARTINUS: No.

GIDEON *(Rage)*: What do you mean "No"? It's a bloody good joke man. "Twenty-seven Swapo cabbages in the garden, daddy!"

MARTINUS: Then why don't you laugh?

GIDEON: You want to hear laughter? I'll give you fucking laughter. *(He makes a violent and grotesque attempt at laughter that spirals away into the sound of his pain and torment. He is left totally defeated)*

MARTINUS *(After a pause)*: No, you are not laughing. *(He speaks quietly, calmly)* What is the matter with you white man? What is it you are doing tonight? You come here to me, but I don't want you. I tell you so, but you come back. You come back again and again. You make bad trouble between us. You try to make me kill you and now you tell me you are laughing at dead men but I can see it is a lie. Why? Why are you telling me that lie? Why are you trying so hard to make me believe it?

Gideon denies nothing.

I remember once when I also tried very hard to tell a lie. It was when I was still small. I broke the window in our house in the location. I was very frightened because my father was a very cross man. So when he came home from work I told him that the other boys playing in the street had done it. I tried very hard to make him believe it. It was no good. He could see my lie and so I got the hiding. When it was finished and I had stopped crying, he said to me, "That was for breaking the window. Now you get another one, a good one, for telling me a lie and trying to hide what really happened." Is that why you are doing it? Are you hiding something away like little Martinus?

(Disturbed by the direction his thoughts are taking)
Aikona! Aikona Martinus! Suka! Leave it now. Go to work. Leave him. His nonsense is not your business.

(He tries to leave) Fuck you white man! I'll see you in Hell. Hey! I said fuck you white man!

No reaction from Gideon. Martinus returns.

Okay. I am going to ask you, but you must tell me no more lies. What is the true feeling inside you?

GIDEON: Leave me alone.

MARTINUS: No, you must tell me now. You must speak the truth. What is the feeling you got inside you?

GIDEON: Feeling? I've got fucking feelings for Africa man. Which ones do you want? Bad feelings, sick feelings, hate feelings?

MARTINUS: Inside you now. Your feelings about what you did. The dead men. Twenty-seven dead men.

GIDEON: No! Leave me alone. I say fuck you to you as well. Go do your work. Go do anything you like—just go. You're right, there's nothing between you and me.

Pause. Martinus decides. He sits.

MARTINUS: Listen to me now. I am going to tell you something else. When I was sitting in the death cell, waiting, the prison dominee came to visit me. Dominee Badenhorst. He came to me every day with his Bible. He read to me about the Commandments—specially Number Six—Thou Shall Not Kill. He said to me, "Martinus, you have sinned. You have killed a man. But if you pray and ask God for Forgiveness and he looks into your heart and sees that you are really sorry, then he will forgive you."

Then I said to him, "But I am not sorry." Then he said, "Then you will go to Hell Martinus."

"I can't help it, Dominee," I said, "then I will go to Hell, but I can't feel sorry."

He wouldn't believe me. "No," he said, "that is not so. You are a good man Martinus. Look deep into your heart. I know you are sorry for what you did."

"Listen Dominee," I said, "I say it to the Judge and now I say it to you also—if I saw that white man tomorrow, I would kill him again. It would make me very very happy to kill him again."

The dominee was very sad and prayed for me. There in the cell, on his knees, he prayed to God to make me feel

ATHOL FUGARD

sorry. But it is no good. I still don't have that feeling. All
the years I was in jail, and all the years I sit here by the fire,
I ask myself, "What is it that makes a man feel sorry? Why
doesn't it happen inside me?" Baas Joppie—he was the
prison carpenter, I was his handlanger—he was sorry. He
killed his father and he was so sorry for doing it he cried all
the times he told me about it. And Jackson Xaba—they
hanged him—guilty four times for rape and murder, he
told me also he was sorry. But me. . . ?

(He shakes his head) The dominee said that if I looked
deep into my heart I would find that feeling. I try. I look
inside. When I sit here every night I look inside and I find
feelings, strong feelings for other things. When I remember
Thandeka and I wonder where she is, I feel a big sadness
inside me. Or when I just sit by the fire when it is cold and
the tea is hot, that makes me feel good inside. Bread and
meat, good! Rain! Rain falling in this dry Karoo—very
good! I even find feelings for dead dogs. But for him—
Andries Jacobus de Lange, the Deceased, the man I
killed—*No*!

And now there is you.

(Again shaking his head in disbelief) You have got that
sorry feeling for what you did, for the men you killed,
haven't you?

Gideon tries to wave him away.

When did it come? When you killed them? Later? When
you counted them?

GIDEON: What difference does it make when it happened? It
happened!

(A voice shorn of all deception) I was too revved up at the
time to feel anything. When you're in the middle of
something like that and you've got your finger on the
trigger of that R3, there's only one thought in your head:

41

You're alive Gid! Keep it that way man. Stay fucking alive.
The only thing going on inside you is a sort of wild feeling,
but I mean like really wild man. And anyway because it
was a follow-up we didn't even rest, so there wasn't time to
think about anything. We just kept on going after them.

We came back that way a few days later. Hell man, it was
terrible. A man starts smelling bad the minute he's dead,
but when he's been lying out in the sun for a few days. . . !
Believe me I wasn't exaggerating when I said you can't eat
your food afterwards. Me and another chap was detailed to
take the bodies and dump them in a big hole. Oh boy!
First we had to load them onto the back of the lorry, one
by one—we had to wear gloves and masks it was so bad—
then we drove over to the hole. When we got there I see
this old woman come out of the bush and stand there and
watch us. She didn't do anything or say anything—she just
stood there watching.

So we back the lorry up to the hole and started. . . . He
grabs the hand, I grab a leg, drag it to the edge and then
. . . into the hole. First you kind of try to do it nicely you
know, because after all they was human beings, but by the
time you get halfway through you just don't give a damn
anymore—it's hot and you're feeling naar so you just chuck
them in. All the time I was doing this I had a strange
feeling that it reminded me of something, but I couldn't
remember what it was. And the old woman was still
standing there watching us. I couldn't take it anymore so I
started shouting and swearing at her, telling her to go away,
and while I was doing that suddenly it came to me, the
thing I was trying to remember.

It was the time we was on holiday at Mossel Bay—me
and my mom and my dad. I was still just a little outjie in a
khaki broek. Every day me and my dad would take his
fishing rod and go down to the rocks. He would put on
some bait and throw out and then wait for a big one. My

job was to catch him the small fishes in the rock pools for
him to use as bait. So one day I catch this lekker fat little
fish and I'm all excited and I start to cut it up and then—
Here! man, hundreds of little babies jump out of its
stomach onto the rock. Just so big . . . *(Indicating with his
fingers)* little babies man!—they already has little black dots
where their eyes was going to be—jumping around there
on the rock. And the mother fish also, with her stomach
hanging open where I had cut her, wagging her tail there
on the rock. And I looked down at all of this and I knew
man, I just knew that what I had done was a terrible sin.
Any way you look at it, whether you believe all that stuff
about Heaven and Hell and God Almighty or not it makes
no difference. What I had done was a sin. You can't do that
to a mother and her babies. I don't care what it is, a fish or
a dog or another person, it's wrong!

So then what the hell was going on man? There I was on
the back of that lorry doing it again. Only this time it was
men I was sommer throwing into that hole. Maybe one of
them was that woman's son. Maybe I had killed him. That
did it. Something just went inside me and it was snot and
tears into that face mask like I never cried in my whole life,
not even when I was small. I tore off the mask and gloves
and got off the lorry and went over to where the old
woman had been standing, but she was gone. I ran into the
bush to try and find her, I looked and called, but she was
gone. That's where they found me the next day. They said I
was just walking around in a dwaal.

MARTINUS: What did you want with the old woman?

GIDEON: I wanted to tell her about that little boy. I wanted to
tell her that he knew what was right and wrong. I don't
know what happened to him, what went wrong in his life,
but he didn't want to grow up to be a man throwing other
men into a hole like rotten cabbages. He didn't want to be
me. And when I had told her all that, I was going to ask

her for forgiveness . . . but she was gone.

A silence between the two men. Martinus finally understands.

MARTINUS: So that is it. That is why you keep coming back tonight. Forgiveness.

GIDEON: Ja.

MARTINUS: For twenty-seven dead men.

GIDEON: Ja.

MARTINUS: How many did you kill?

GIDEON: Doesn't make any difference man. You killed one, you killed them all.

MARTINUS: Number Six twenty-seven times! And you say there was also other times?

GIDEON: Ja.

MARTINUS: No! That's too big for me white man. I'm just a night watchman. Go ask God for that forgiveness.

GIDEON: Forget about Him man. He's forgotten about us. It's me and you tonight. The whole world is me and you. Here! Now!

   (Anger and bitterness) Do you think I wanted it to be this way? Do you think that if I could have chosen the other person in my world tonight it would be you? No such luck. We've got no choices man. I've got you and you've got me. Finish and klaar. Forgive me or kill me. That's the only choice you've got.

MARTINUS: If I forgive you, then I must forgive Andries Jacobus de Lange, and if I forgive him, then I must ask God to forgive me . . . and then what is left? Nothing! I sit here with nothing . . . tonight . . . tomorrow . . . all my days and all my nights . . . nothing! *(Violent rejection)* No! It's too late to talk forgiveness to me. It's like you say, it's all finish and klaar now. We've done what we've done. Number Six—you and me. So leave it alone. We go to Hell and that is the end of it.

(Pause. It is his moment of defeat) Haai white man! Why did you bring me so much trouble tonight? Forgive you or kill you! What do I know about forgiveness? Nothing. My heart knows how to hate Andries Jacobus de Lange. That is all it can do. But kill you? No. I don't know if I can do it again.

I know I have only killed one man, but I have done it too many many times. Every night when I sit here I wait again in that little room in the backyard. I wait again in the dark with my knife, I wait for him and when he comes I kill him—again and again—too many times.

GIDEON: Ja. I know what you're saying. It burns you out hey? Kill somebody and sooner or later you end up like one of those landmine wrecks on the side of the road up there on the Border—burnt-out and bloody useless.

So where the hell did it go wrong man? Because it wasn't meant to be like this. Isn't that so? I mean, did you want to spend your whole life like you just said—hating one man and spooking with him every night in that little room where you killed him?

MARTINUS: No. I wanted to do other things with my life.

GIDEON: I didn't want to spend mine hating myself. But look at me. That's all I do now. Everything else is just pretending. I try to make it look as if I'm getting on with things like everybody else: I wake up, go to work, joke with the other ous, argue with the foreman, go home, eat supper, watch TV with my ma . . . but it's all a lie man. Inside me I'm still at that hole outside Oshakati. That's where I go every bloody night in my dreams—looking for that old woman in the bush . . . and never finding her.

(Parodying himself) "You're alive Gid!"

What a bloody joke. I'm as dead as the men I buried and I'm also spooking the place where I did it.

Pause. First light of the new day.

45

It's getting light. Hell, have we been talking that long?

MARTINUS: Ja, we've been talking long.

GIDEON: I can see you now. Yessus, you're an ugly bugger.

MARTINUS: You too.

GIDEON: This is about the time when me and my dad use to wake up, get dressed and then go open the hok and let them out—even in winter—early morning, just before sunrise. Then we would go back into the kitchen and make our coffee and take it out into the backyard and watch them flying around. Sometimes they was up there in the sunlight, while we were still in the shadows! It always made us laugh. I don't know why, but we would just stand there, drink our coffee, watch the dawn maneuvers of the Karoo Squadron . . . and laugh our bloody heads off. And there were no lies in that laugh. It was for real. That was how we felt inside.

So. . . ?

Martinus is silent.

That's it then. New Day. New Year. Did I wish you Happy New Year last night?

MARTINUS: No.

GIDEON: Well better late than never as they say. Happy New Year to you and . . . what else? . . . Ja, thanks for the chat.

An awkward, hesitant moment between the two men. Gideon starts to leave.

MARTINUS *(Impulsively and with conviction)*: To hell with it! I have got something to say.

GIDEON: What!

MARTINUS: I also want to see them. Those pigeon-birds. Flying round up there like you say. I also want to see that.

GIDEON: What are you saying man?

MARTINUS: I am saying to you that when Playland comes back
here next time—Christmas and New Year—I want to do it
like you said . . . look up in the sky, watch the pigeon-birds
flying and drink my tea and laugh!

GIDEON: Do you mean that?

MARTINUS: I am saying it to you because I mean it. To hell with
spooking! You are alive. So go home and do it. Get some
planks, find some nails and a hammer and fix that hok.
Start again with the pigeon-birds.

    (Pause) Do you hear what I am saying Gideon le Roux?

GIDEON: I hear you Martinus Zoeloe.

MARTINUS: Do you understand what I am saying?

GIDEON: Ja. I think so.

    And you also hey. Get out of that little room man. Let
old Andries spook there by himself tonight. Do you
understand me Martinus Zoeloe?

MARTINUS: Ja. I understand you.

GIDEON: Good.

    And to prove that you are alive and not a spook come
give me a push man. I know that bloody tjorrie of mine is
not going to start again. Been giving me trouble all bloody
week. I don't know what is wrong with it. Been into the
garage two times already this month . . .

They walk off together.

GLOSSARY

aikona!: no!

baas: boss or master

bakgat: great

Bantu: official term for black South Africans and their
  language, disliked by black people

Base Camp Oshakati: principal camp of South African
  defense during the Border War; near the border of what
  used to be South West Africa and is now Namibia

Boere: from "boer" meaning "country" or "farmer"; often
  used in compound words; *Boere dogs*, hot dogs;
  Boeremusiek, country music

bosbefok: rude term meaning "shell-shocked"

boskak: wild shit

braaivleis: barbecue

broek: pants; trousers

buitengewoon: out of the ordinary

dop: a swig of hard liquor

dwaal: daze

eina: ouch!

ek is moeg: I'm worn out

gat: ass; *gat-full*, up to my ass

haai: no

handlanger: handyman

Here!: Lord! Christ!

hok: cage for pigeons

ja: yes

japie: dolt; bumpkin

kak: shit

Karoo: southern desert region of South Africa

kêrel: fellow; chap

kierie: fighting stick

klaar: finished; ready

klaarstaan: be ready or cautious

lekker: nice

location: township; black ghetto

naar: nauseated

ou: common mode of address to man or boy; chap

ou bollie: old man

oubaas: old man

outjie: boy; little guy

poephol: farthole

rand: South African money

se gat: ass's

skeel oog: squint eye

skelm: rascal

skollies: bums

sommer: just; simply

suka: stop!

tjorrie: old, small car

verneuk the baas: rip-off the boss

voetsek: fuck off

A PLACE
WITH THE
PIGS

A Place with the Pigs was originally produced by Yale Repertory Theatre (Lloyd Richards, Artistic Director), in New Haven, Connecticut on March 24, 1987, under the direction of the playwright. Set design was by Ann Sheffield, costume design by Susan Hilferty, lighting design by Michael Chybowski and sound design by David Budries. The cast was as follows:

Pavel   *Athol Fugard*
Praskovya   *Suzanne Shepherd*

CHARACTERS
PAVEL
PRASKOVYA

PLACE
A pigsty, in a small village,
somewhere in the author's imagination.

NOTE
The writing of this play was provoked by the true story of Pavel
Ivanovich Navrotsky, a deserter from the Soviet army in the
Second World War, who spent forty-one years of self-imposed
exile in a pigsty.

SCENE 1

The Anniversary of the Great Victory

A pigsty, in a small village, somewhere in the author's imagination. A dank, unwholesome world. One of the pens has been converted into a primitive living area . . . only bare essentials . . . but all of them obviously already in use for quite a few years. Walls are covered with an attempt to keep track of the passing of time: bundles of six strokes with another one across for the seven days of the week, the weeks and necessary odd days circled into months, the months blocked off into years . . . 1944 to 1954. It is a noisy, restless period in the sty— the pigs are waiting to be fed—a cacophony of grunts, squeals and other swinish sounds. Pavel Ivanovich Navrotsky is in the living area. He is in his mid-thirties, a desperate, haunted-looking individual. He is busy with pencil and paper trying to rehearse a speech.

PAVEL: "Comrades, Pavel Ivanovich Navrotsky is not dead. He is alive. It is he who stands before you. I beg you, listen to his story and then deal with him as you see fit. Comrades, I also beg you to believe that it is a deeply repentant man who speaks . . ." *(He can hardly hear himself above the noise from the pigs. He speaks louder)* ". . . that it is a deeply

repentant man who speaks these words to you . . ." SHUT
UP! *(He grabs a stick and rushes around the sty, lashing out at
the pigs)* Silence, you filthy bastards! I want silence! Silence!
Silence!

*Squeals and then a slight abatement of noise. Pavel returns to
his speech.*

"Comrades, I also beg you to believe that it is a deeply
repentant man who speaks these words to you and who
acknowledges the error of his ways . . . *(Making a
correction)* . . . acknowledges in full his guilt. I, Pavel
Ivanovich Navrotsky, ask only that in your judgment of
me . . . *(Another correction)* . . . ask only that in deciding on
my punishment, for I have already judged myself and
found myself guilty, I ask only that you temper that
punishment with mercy."

The pigs are starting up again. Pavel goes to a door.

Praskovya! Praskovya! *(No reply)* Praskovya!
PRASKOVYA *(A distant voice)*: I'm coming . . . I'm coming!
PAVEL: Well, hurry up.

Praskovya appears, burdened with buckets of pigswill.

PRASKOVYA: I'm coming as fast as I can.
PAVEL: You're late.
PRASKOVYA: I'm not, Pavel.
PAVEL: Don't argue with me, woman! Listen to them. They're
    going berserk. I can't hear myself think in here.
PRASKOVYA: All right then, I'm late.
PAVEL: Well then, get on with it, Praskovya . . . feed them! You
    appear to have forgotten that in just a few hours' time I

face the severest, the single most decisive test of my entire life.

PRASKOVYA: I know that, Pavel.

PAVEL: I find that hard to believe.

PRASKOVYA: God only gave me two arms and two legs, and I've been working them since I woke up this morning as if I'd been sentenced to hard labor. If you're interested in the truth, Pavel, I'm feeding the pigs an hour earlier than usual so that I will be free to give you all the attention and help I can.

PAVEL *(Back with his speech)*: "Comrades! Standing before you is a miserable wretch of a man, a despicable, weak creature worthy of nothing but your contempt. In his defence, I say only that if you had witnessed the years of mental anguish, of spiritual torment, which he has inflicted on himself in judgment of himself, then I know, Comrades, that the impulse in your noble and merciful hearts would be: 'He has suffered enough. Let him go.' For ten years he has been imprisoned by his own conscience in circumstances which would make the most hardened among you wince. Yes, for ten years . . ." *(His voice trails off into silence. Wandering around the sty)* Ten years! Has it really been ten years?

PRASKOVYA: Yes.

PAVEL: Not nine?

PRASKOVYA: No.

PAVEL: Or eleven?

PRASKOVYA: No.

Pavel is counting the years as blocked out on the walls.

You've checked it and double-checked it a dozen times already, Pavel.

PAVEL: Yes . . . ten years, two months and six days to be precise. There it is! *(Stepping back with pride as an artist would from his canvas)* Nobody can argue with that, can they? "There, Comrades, count it for yourselves . . . every day of my self-imposed banishment from the human race!"

PRASKOVYA: Sometimes, coming in here to feed you and them, it feels as if we've been at it for twenty.

PAVEL: Only twenty? Is that your worst? I've had days when it felt as if I'd been in here a hundred years. Two hundred! I've already lived through centuries of it. You must understand, Praskovya, life in here has involved dealing with two realities, two profound philosophic realities which have dominated my entire existence, permeated every corner of my being . . . Pig Shit and Time. Just as my body and every one of its senses has had to deal with Pig Shit . . . smelling it, feeling, tasting it . . . just so my soul has had to reckon with Time . . . leaden-footed little seconds, sluggish minutes, reluctant hours, tedious days, monotonous months and then, only then, the years crawling past like old tortoises.

PRASKOVYA: You must tell that to the comrades, Pavel.

PAVEL: I intend to.

PRASKOVYA: It sounds very impressive.

PAVEL *(His speech)*: Oh yes, don't worry . . . I intend to draw a very vivid picture of what I have had to endure in here right from that very first night.

PRASKOVYA: It was a Sunday night. Your first night in here.

PAVEL: I don't think the actual day is all that important.

PRASKOVYA: Just mentioning it, in case you're interested in the truth. I know it for certain because the storm had kept me from church and I was trying to make up for it before going to bed by saying my prayers a second time, and then a third . . . when I heard the scratching at the door.

Pavel's attention is riveted by her memories of that most decisive night in his life. Encouraged by his attention she continues.

At first I thought it was just a poor dog trying to find shelter from the blizzard. But then came the tapping at the window! Oh dear me, I thought, no dog can reach up there, not even on its hind legs! Suppose it's a big black bear! And when I peeped through the curtains . . . Mother of God! . . . that is what I thought I saw, what you looked like . . . all hair and beard and muffled up in your big coat with the snow swirling behind you. But when you tapped again I saw your hand, so I unbolted the door and let you in. But even then it took me some minutes to realize that the pathetic creature I was looking at was you, Pavel. You should have seen yourself.

PAVEL *(Greedy for still more)*: Yes yes yes . . .

PRASKOVYA: Your lips were blue, your fingers frozen stiff. You could hardly hold the mug of soup I tried to get you to drink. I had to feed you like a baby. And then, when your tongue had thawed out enough for your first words . . . *(She shakes her head in disbelief)*

PAVEL: Yes yes . . .

PRASKOVYA: You asked for your slippers!

PAVEL: Go on.

PRASKOVYA: And then when I brought them to you, when you saw them, you broke down and started crying. Clutching them to your breast and sobbing. . . . Oh, Pavel! Sobbing in a way that nearly broke my heart! . . . You got up, staggered out of the house and collapsed in here.

Pavel fetches a small bundle which has been carefully hidden away somewhere in the living area. He sits down at the table and, after wiping his hands clean on his shirt, reverently unwraps it. He produces a pair of slippers.

PAVEL: Oh, dear God! Every time I touch them, or just look at them . . . sometimes when I even just think about them . . . a flood of grief and guilt wrecks my soul as it did

that night ten years ago. Look, Praskovya, look . . . do you
see? . . . little flowers and birds.

PRASKOVYA: The needlework is very fine.

PAVEL: My mother's hands!

PRASKOVYA: And what a clever pair of hands they were. *(Still
admiring the slippers)* And just look at the colors, still so
bright and fresh! You should wear them, Pavel. One day the
rats are going to find them.

PAVEL: Wear them? In here? How can you suggest such a thing!
That would be sacrilege. No, my conscience will not allow
me to wear these until the day when I am once again a free
man. That is my most solemn vow! *(A little flutter of hope)*
And who knows, Praskovya, this could be that day.
Listen . . .

*In the distance we hear the sound of a brass brand—the
discordancies of individual instruments being warmed up.*

The band has arrived! They're getting ready. *(Pause, then
quietly)* During the war, at the front, deserters weren't even
given a trial. Just forced to their knees and then a bullet in
the back of the head. I saw it . . . blood, bright red blood
on the snow. *(Putting his papers in order)* Pray for me,
Praskovya.

PRASKOVYA: I already have.

PAVEL: Then pray again . . . pray harder! Bully God with your
prayers. I don't just deserve mercy, I've earned it!

PRASKOVYA: I will be down on my knees, Pavel, praying harder
than I have ever prayed in my life from that moment you
walk out that door and leave me. But, for the last time,
Pavel, are you quite sure you are doing the right thing?

PAVEL: Yes yes YES! Let's go over the ceremony once more.

PRASKOVYA: Again?

PAVEL: Yes, a hundred times again, if necessary. For God's sake,
Praskovya, my life is at stake.

PRASKOVYA: Everybody has been told to gather in the village square at ten o'clock. The ceremony will start with the arrival of the Ex-Soldiers' Brigade, the Young Pioneers and the Collective Fire Brigade. They are going to march through the village along the route taken by our troops on the glorious day of the liberation ten years ago. When everybody has settled down, we will all join in singing the Hymn of the Revolution. This will be followed by words of welcome from the Village Chairman and the reading of a message from the Central Committee in Moscow. Then the singing of the Victory Anthem, which brings us to the grand climax . . . Comrade Secretary Chomski's speech and the unveiling of the monument. After the unveiling, the School Principal will read out the names of the gallant dead, and with each name, the widow, mother or daughter of the departed will step forward and lay her wreath at the foot of the monument . . .

PAVEL: Which is when I will make my move! I will stay hidden at the back of the crowd until the reading of the names, but when they reach mine . . . *I* will step forward and declare myself. "Comrades, Pavel Ivanovich Navrotsky is not dead. He is alive. It is he who stands here before you. I beg you, listen to his story and then deal with him as you see fit."

PRASKOVYA: I'm frightened, Pavel.

PAVEL: You're frightened! How do you think I feel? I'm the one who is going to be standing up there with a thousand pairs of eyes staring at me, judging me.

PRASKOVYA: Suppose something goes wrong?

PAVEL *(Hanging on)*: Nothing is going to go wrong.

PRASKOVYA: I think you may have forgotten what this village is like, Pavel. There are going to be some mean and uncharitable souls out there.

PAVEL: We've already had this discussion, Praskovya . . . and we agreed that the ceremony and the music and the speeches will have an elevating influence on their thoughts and feelings. . . . They will have been lifted up to a higher plane. . . . They will be forgiving . . .

PRASKOVYA *(Who has her doubts)*: Boris Ratnitski forgiving? Or old Arkadina Petrovna? She packed off a husband, two brothers and three sons to the war and not one of them came back. They say she's got a picture of Hitler somewhere in her house which she spits on every morning when she wakes up.

PAVEL *(A cry of despair)*: Praskovya! Praskovya! I am trying to hold on to what little courage I have left in my bruised and battered soul. Don't destroy it! Give me support, woman! *(He calms down)* There is no other way. This is my only chance. The alternative *is* madness . . . or suicide! I mean it, Praskovya. One more day in here, and I'll cut my throat! *(Steadying himself)* But that is not going to be necessary, because I have prepared a very moving and eloquent plea to the comrades. I promise you, Praskovya, there will not be many dry eyes out there by the time I am finished. *(The papers for his speech)* Where is it? . . . Where is it? . . . Yes . . . listen: ". . . dark nights of despair from which the next day's dawn brought no release. . . ." And what about this: "Remorse was the bitter bread of my soul in its cold, gray and foul-smelling entombment. . . ." Many was the time you yourself said I could have made a career of the stage if I had wanted to. Well, Fate has done it. Today I must give the performance of and for my life. And I am ready for it, Praskovya. *(His speech)* When I stand there in front of them in my uniform, the truth and sincerity of these words will strike home.

PRASKOVYA: Stand there in your what?

PAVEL: My uniform . . . as Comrade Private Pavel Ivanovich Navrotsky, first class, of the Sarazhentsy Brigade . . .

PRASKOVYA: Pavel . . .

PAVEL: They won't see me as an enemy . . .

PRASKOVYA: Pavel . . .

PAVEL: . . . to be punished for his desertion and betrayal of the Cause. Oh no . . .

PRASKOVYA: Pavel!!

She finally manages to silence him.

I have got your suit, your fine black suit shaken out and aired and all ready for you.

PAVEL: My suit?

PRASKOVYA: Yes. Don't you remember? You got married in it.

PAVEL: Of course I remember it. But I'm going to wear my uniform.

PRASKOVYA: Pavel, please . . .

PAVEL: We haven't got time for pointless arguments, Praskovya. Don't you understand anything? I'm *surrendering*. A soldier does not surrender in the fine black suit he got married in.

PRASKOVYA: Please listen to me, Pavel . . .

PAVEL: No! Why are you making it so hard for me, Praskovya! Do I have to argue with you and fight about everything? I've had enough of it now. Just do as I say. Go and fetch my uniform. Praskovya! Move!

A leaden-footed Praskovya leaves the sty.

(Washing himself) Courage, Pavel. Courage! It's nearly over. One way or the other this purgatory is nearly at an end. *(A farewell circuit of the pens)* Did you hear that my darlings? I'll be leaving you soon. Yes, my little shit-eaters, you'll have to find another victim to torment with your bestiality. So, in memory of the years we have shared in here, Pavel Ivanovich will leave you with one last gesture of his deep, oh so deep and abiding loathing and disgust.

He grabs his stick and brutalizes the pigs, striking and prodding them viciously. The exercise affords him considerable

*satisfaction. An exhausted and happy Pavel retires to his living
area. Praskovya returns. In terrified silence she hands over to
the still manic and panting Pavel a miserable little bundle. He
unwraps it. It produces a few moth-eaten remnants of his
uniform . . . cap, torn old tunic, one legging, etc., etc.*

What's this?

PRASKOVYA: I tried to tell you.

PAVEL: Praskovya. . . ?

PRASKOVYA: That's it. And you're lucky there is that much left
of it. When you gave it to me you said I must burn it, but I
thought that was a wasteful thing to do with such a good
bundle of rags, because that is all it was . . . so I just stuffed
it away in a corner and whenever I needed one . . . *(Her
voice trails off)* I never dreamt you would ever need it again.

PAVEL *(Stunned disbelief)*: Are you telling me that this. . . . No!
It can't be. You are not telling me that, are you?

PRASKOVYA: Yes.

PAVEL: Yes, what?

PRASKOVYA: Yes, that *is* what I'm telling you.

PAVEL: That this . . .

PRASKOVYA: . . . is your uniform . . . what is left of it.

PAVEL: But the buttons . . . shiny brass buttons . . . six of them,
all the way down here in the front.

PRASKOVYA: There were no buttons left when you came home
that night.

PAVEL: Are you sure?

PRASKOVYA: Yes.

Stunned silence from Pavel as he examines the rags.

I'm afraid the mice have had a little nibble as well.

Pavel slips on what is left of his tunic. Praskovya shakes her

*head. He puts on the cap and salutes. Praskovya shakes her
head again.*

Somebody might laugh.

Pavel is devastated.

Take my advice and wear your suit. It's all ready for you. A
clean white shirt. And I've given your black shoes a really
good polish . . . shining like mirrors they are. It won't make
all that much difference surely. So instead of Private
Navrotsky the soldier, they'll see responsible, sober, law-
abiding Comrade Pavel Ivanovich they all remember so
well. It might even work to your advantage.

PAVEL: For God's sake, Praskovya! Didn't you hear me? This is a
military occasion. A deserter does not appear before his
court martial in his wedding suit. "Why aren't you in
uniform, Private Navrotsky?" "Comrade Sergeant, my wife
used it to mop the floor, and then the mice and the moths
made a meal of what was left." That is sure to save me from
the firing squad! *(Doubts begin)* No . . . no . . . wait . . . let
me think . . . let me think. *(Agitated pacing)* This calls for
very careful thought . . . a reappraisal of the situation in the
light of new and unexpected developments. There has got
to be a simple solution . . . which we will find, provided we
stay calm and don't panic. *(Pause. His nerve is beginning to
fail)* Suppose I'm wrong, Praskovya.

PRASKOVYA: About what?

PAVEL: Them . . . *(A gesture to the world outside)* Suppose my
innocent faith in human nature, my trusting belief in the
essential goodness of our comrades' hearts . . . *(Swallows)* is
a big, big mistake. That instead of forgiveness and
understanding, when they hear my story . . . maybe . . . just
maybe . . . they will hate and despise me. See in me and my

moment of weakness ten years ago, a reminder of *their* own
weaknesses . . . weaknesses they do not wish to confess to or
be reminded of. Because you are certainly right about one
thing, Praskovya Alexandrovna . . . that is not an assembly
of saints out there clearing their throats for the singing of
the anthem. Oh, most certainly not. If the truth be known
about some of our respectable comrades out there, I
wouldn't be the only one pleading for mercy today. My
theory about the elevation of their thoughts and feelings
onto a higher plane is dependent on there being enough
basic humanity left in them to allow that to happen. But as
you so perceptively pointed out, Praskovya, knowing some
of them, that amounts to asking for a small miracle.
(Hitting his head) Stupid! Stupid! Stupid! I've been in here
so long, I've forgotten what human nature is really like.
Compassion and forgiveness? I stand as much chance of
getting that from the mob out there as I do from these pigs.

The brass band is now in full swing.

PRASKOVYA: So what is it going to be, Pavel? They sound just
about ready. It's now or never.
(Pause) Did you hear me, Pavel? It's time to go. Are you
still going out there?
PAVEL *(Very small and very frightened)*: I can't. It's no good,
Praskovya . . . I just can't. I won't get a fair trial. They won't
even give me a hearing. The moment I appear they'll throw
themselves on me and tear me apart like a pack of Siberian
wolves. *(He throws away the papers for his speech)*
PRASKOVYA: So this is the end of it, then.
PAVEL: For me it is. You are the one who must give the
performance now.
PRASKOVYA: Me?
PAVEL: Yes. So prepare yourself.
PRASKOVYA: What do you mean?

PAVEL: Your black dress . . . and didn't you say something about
flowers? . . . A funeral wreath! When you hear my
name . . . weep, Praskovya . . . weep! Because your Pavel is
now as good as in his grave.

PRASKOVYA *(Nervous)*: You want me to go out there . . . in
front of all those people . . . and pretend you're dead.

PAVEL: Isn't that what you've been doing for the past ten years?

PRASKOVYA: Yes, that's true . . . but not on such a grand scale,
Pavel. Widow's weeds and flowers, with a brass band
playing!

PAVEL: Are you trying to get out of it?

PRASKOVYA: Yes! NO! If you want me to go out there, Pavel,
I'll do it. But I want you to know that I'm as frightened of
going out there as you are. You don't seem to realize that I
hardly see anybody anymore. The only dealings I have with
the outside world now is when I take one of the pigs down
to the butcher. For the rest, I'm as much a prisoner in the
house as you are in here.

PAVEL: You're wasting time, Praskovya. If you're not out there
ready to step forward when my name is called, people will
get suspicious and start asking questions.

She is very reluctant to move.

I'm warning you, at this rate you will end up mourning my
real death before the day is over.

PRASKOVYA: All right, all right . . . I'm going. But I'm telling
you, Pavel, this feels like a big, bad sin. Hiding you was one
thing, but what you're asking me to do now. . . !!

*She exits, shaking her head with misgivings. The brass band is
now playing away vigorously in the distance.*

PAVEL *(With the slippers)*: Oh, Mama! These did it. It's all
wrong, I know, because you made them with such love for

your little Pavel, but if you could see what they have done to him, you would rise from your grave and curse the day you stitched them together. *(A helpless gesture)* It all seemed so simple at first! They gave me a uniform and a gun, taught me how to salute and then on a fine spring day, I kissed Praskovya goodbye and marched off with the others to win the war. And the thought of these *(The slippers)*, waiting for me at home, kept me going . . . kept me smiling and whistling away even when the marches were forced and long. At first the others teased me about them. But as the weeks passed and we tramped further and further away from home, they eventually stopped laughing. The time came, when sitting around at night with no songs left to sing or jokes to tell, sooner or later one of them would say in a small voice: "Hey, Pavel, tell us about your slippers." The men would stare into the fire with sad, homesick eyes while I talked about them, about slipping my feet into their cozy padded comfort and settling down next to the stove with Praskovya, to talk about the weather or the pigs or the latest village gossip . . . the silly unimportant little things that break a big man's heart when he is far away from home.

That first winter wasn't too bad. "Next spring," we said, trying to cheer each other up, "we'll be back home next spring." We even managed somehow to get through the second one with our spirits still intact. But a year later, there we were, once again, watching the first snow fall, and our victorious march back home seemed even further away than ever. And what a winter that one turned out to be, Mama! The oldest among us could not remember snow that deep or temperatures that low . . . winds so sharp and cold the skin blistered and cracked open to the bone. Our hands could barely hold the pitiful crusts of bread we were given as rations. And for what? Why were we all dying of hunger and cold when we had warm homes and young wives waiting for us? The stupidity of it all made me want to vomit up food I didn't have in my belly. That is when they *(The slippers)* lost their innocence and began to torment me. Sitting there huddled in the trench, an image of them would come floating into my deranged mind . . . and with them, smells and sounds . . . of pine logs cracking and hissing away in the stove . . . crusty warm bread and freshly churned butter. . . . Weak as I was, I might still have been able to cope with that, but then the little voice started whispering. "Go home, Pavel Ivanovich, go home." I tried to shut my ears to it with prayers and patriotic songs, but nothing helped. It just carried on . . . laughing at me and my faltering loyalty, mocking all that was sacred. . . . "There are no flags in either heaven or hell, no causes beyond the grave." And always the same refrain. "Go home, Pavel Ivanovich, your slippers are waiting for you. Go home!"

In the distance the brass band and voices singing.

Am I such a terrible sinner, Mama, for having yielded to temptation under those circumstances . . . half-crazed as I was with hunger and cold? One night . . . all I wanted was one more night beside the stove in these slippers, and then I would have happily laid down my life defending our Motherland. But when I came to my senses in here, Praskovya told me that a month had already passed. One day, one week, one month. . . ! It would have all come to the same thing in the end . . . one bullet in the back of the head.

An excited and happy Praskovya bursts into the sty. She is now dressed in black and carries her Bible and a small Russian flag.

PRASKOVYA: Pasha . . . Pasha. . . . It's all right, Pasha. It's all over and it's all right. Do you want to hear about it, Pavel?

He stares at her in silence. She produces a little black box.

To start with, you've been awarded a medal . . . for making
the Supreme Sacrifice . . . *(The inscription on the medal)*
"Pavel Ivanovich Navrotsky. A Hero of the People." Your
mother would have been so proud. Your name is also
inscribed on the monument. As for Comrade Secretary
Chomski's speech. . . . You did the right thing after all,
Pavel, in not going out there. You would have had a hard
time making an appearance after what he had to say. He
started off by urging all of us . . . "sons and daughters of
the Glorious Revolution" . . . to take a lesson in self-
sacrifice and dedication to the Cause from the noble
comrades whose names have been chiselled in granite for
all future generations to read. The world we live in is safe,
Pavel, thanks to the likes of you . . . "the Russian bears who
mauled the fascist mongrels" . . . our children, and their
children, and their children's children, will grow up in a
world of plenty for all, thanks to the likes of you . . . the
brave fifty of Sarazhentsy who sacrificed their lives
defending the Revolution in the Winter Campaign of '43.
And finally, the fact that you lie somewhere in an
unmarked grave doesn't really matter, because your
memory is enshrined forever in the hearts of the People.
(She pins the medal to Pavel's chest)
   As for our comrades out there . . . a sight to behold!
They wept for you, Pavel, as if you were their very own
flesh and blood. When I returned to my place after laying
my flowers, I thought I was going to end up bruised all
over from the embraces I got for "our beloved Pavel
Ivanovich." I'm not exaggerating. That old skinflint
Smetalov . . . he buried his bald head in those money-
grabbing paws of his and wept! All of them . . . Tamara,

Galina, Nastasia . . . every single one of them had the chance for a really good cry thanks to you. There would have been a lot of disappointed people out there if you had cut short that grief with an unexpected appearance. But do you want to know what is strangest of all, Pavel? There was a time out there when I myself was so overcome with emotion at the thought of your lonely and bitter death so far away from home, that I also started to cry! Yes! Under the power of Comrade Secretary Chomski's words, for some minutes I myself believed that you were dead. Look! I'm ready to start again. *(Wiping away her tears)* But that still isn't the end of it. I don't mean to upset you, but it will be on my conscience unless I tell you. When it was all over, Smetalov insisted on walking back with me, and on the way . . . he proposed to me. At least that is what I think he was doing. "The joyful vision of my pigs and his cows under the same roof" . . . is how he put it. He said it would be a happy ending to the sad story of the Widow Navrotsky. I couldn't get rid of him! He's coming back next week for an answer. *(She makes the sign of the cross)* Lord have mercy on us. . . . Our souls will surely roast in Hell for what we have done today. And if our comrades ever find out, we'll be in for a double dose of it. We have lied to them, Pavel . . . publicly! We have made fools of them and a mockery of the anniversary celebrations. Now they will never forgive us.

PAVEL: How is it possible! Like the pigs, all I do in here is eat, sleep and defecate, yet my burden of guilt grows heavier, and heavier. Instead of being diminished by my suffering, it seems to draw nourishment from it . . . like those mushrooms that flourish and get fat on the filth in here. Has it finally come to that, Praskovya? Is my soul now nothing more than a pigsty?

PRASKOVYA: That sounds like a theological question, Pavel. I don't think I know enough to take it on.

PAVEL: Does ten years of human misery count for nothing in the Divine Scales of Justice?

PRASKOVYA: I think it would be wiser if I left that one alone as well. These are all matters beyond my simple woman's head. I will leave you to deal with them. *(She gets up to go)*

PAVEL: Where are you going?

PRASKOVYA: Get changed and then back to work. Celebrations are over. There are chores waiting for me in the house.

PAVEL *(Staring at her, dumbfounded)*: Just like that?

PRASKOVYA: Just like what?

PAVEL: You are going to walk away from me, leave me in here . . . just like that.

PRASKOVYA: Life goes on, Pavel.

PAVEL: Whose life?

PRASKOVYA: Everybody's, I suppose.

PAVEL: Mine as well?

PRASKOVYA: Yes. I pray to God that it goes on as well.

PAVEL *(Crude sarcasm)*: Thank you very much for that information, Praskovya. So, my life is going to go on! How wonderful! Just think of all the challenging possibilities that lie ahead of me in here. The fact that the pigs will be my only company makes the prospect even more exciting, doesn't it? *(Rubbing his hands together in mock relish)* So what should it be? Something in the line of religion? I'm being serious! Maybe there are souls worth saving inside those little mountains of lard. I'll coax them out. Give them all good Christian names and preach the Gospel. St. Pavel of the Pigs! You don't like that? Then what about politics? Yes, that's a possibility as well. This pigsty is a very political situation. In those poor, dumb creatures we might have the last truly underprivileged and exploited working class of the world. I could embrace their cause, become a subversive element and breed rebellion. So that when next you try to lead some poor helpless comrade off to the butcher, you find a small revolution on your hands. Have I

overlooked any possibilities? Please say something before
you go off to peel potatoes or scrub the floors . . .

PRASKOVYA: The potatoes are already peeled . . . I did that first
thing this morning . . . and none of the floors need
scrubbing. If you're interested in the truth, Pavel, there is a
pile of dirty clothes waiting for me. This is washday. So get
ready for it. . . . I am going to walk away from you.

PAVEL: Just like that.

PRASKOVYA: Just like that.

*Exit Praskovya. Pavel alone. The pigs grunting away
contentedly.*

SCENE 2

Beauty and the Beast

*The pigsty. A lot of time has passed. Once again a chorus of pig
noises initiates the scene. Pavel is slumped in mindless apathy.
He is swatting flies with what looks suspiciously like the last
remnant of one of his cherished slippers. The other is on one of
his feet. After a few minutes of this he sweeps together all the
dead flies and counts them. That done, he gets up and goes
over to a wall where we now see that his calendar of days has
been defaced by a tally of dead flies. The score at the moment:
9,762. He adds 23 to this, bringing the total up to 9,785. A few
vacant seconds as he stands scratching himself. His next move
is to take up his stick and go around the sty tormenting the
pigs—a pastime he pursues without either enthusiasm or joy.
In the middle of this he stops suddenly and stares in disbelief: A
butterfly has somehow managed to get into the sty. His mood
slowly undergoes a total transformation as he watches it flutter
around. He is ravished by its beauty, reminding him as it does
of an almost forgotten world of sunlight and flowers, a world*

he now hasn't seen for many, many years. Suppressed calls for Praskovya. He decides to catch the butterfly. A hurried search for something to use as a net . . . he decides on his slipper. He hurries back in search of the butterfly . . . a few seconds of panic when he can't find it . . . ecstatic relief and laughter when he does. He stalks it like a hunter, clambering in and out of pens, but it keeps eluding him. His laughter grows and grows. He stops suddenly.

PAVEL *(Addressing himself with disbelief)*: What is this? Can it be true? Are you laughing, Pavel Ivanovich? *(Answering himself with conviction)* Yes, good comrade. That is perfectly true. I'm trying to catch a butterfly . . . and I'm laughing. *(Which he does with renewed abandon)* Praskovya! I'm laughing! *(Back to the butterfly, his slipper ready)* We must get you out of here, my dainty darling. This is no place for a little beauty like you. Where are you? Little fluttering friend, where are you? Please . . . oh, dear God! . . . *please* don't die in here. Let me give you back to the day outside, to the flowers and the summer breeze . . . and then in return take, oh, I beg you! . . . take just one little whisper of my soul with you into the sunlight. Be my redemption! Ha!!

He sees it and freezes . . . it has settled in one of the pens. Pavel approaches cautiously, ready to pounce. Once again a sudden stop, his eyes widening with horror at the prospect of impending disaster.

No . . . don't . . . no . . . NO!

He is too late. A pig eats the butterfly. He goes berserk with rage.

Murderer! Murderer!

Grabbing a knife, he jumps into the pen and after a furious struggle kills the pig. Terrible gurgles and death squeals from the unfortunate animal. Praskovya bursts in to find a bloodstained, sobbing Pavel.

PRASKOVYA: Pavel . . . Pavel. . . !

PAVEL: Too late . . . too late . . .

PRASKOVYA *(Sees him)*: Oh, my God! What happened? Have you tried to kill yourself? *(She examines him frantically)*

PAVEL *(Still sobbing)*: No . . . no . . .

PRASKOVYA: This isn't your blood?

PAVEL: My soul, Praskovya . . . it's my soul that bleeds.

PRASKOVYA: Well then, there is something else in here bleeding in the old-fashioned way. *(She follows a trail of blood back to the pen and sees the dead pig)* Oh, dear me, just look at her! Did you do that, Pavel? *(She is very impressed)* And all by yourself!

Praskovya fetches a bucket of water and a rag and helps the still distraught Pavel to clean himself.

What happened? Come now . . . tell me all about it and then you'll feel better.

PAVEL *(Collecting himself)*: A butterfly, Praskovya . . . a happy, harmless little beauty with rusty-red wings . . . remember them? From our childhood? . . . Skipping among the blue cornflowers . . .

PRASKOVYA: Oh yes, I remember those!

PAVEL: Well, one of them found its way in here somehow . . . I was busy chastising the pigs when I suddenly saw it fluttering around. I thought to myself, "Oh dear, this is no place for a little butterfly to be. Let me catch it so that Praskovya can set it free outside." Which is what I then tried to do. But . . . the strangest thing, Praskovya! While I was chasing it . . . *(A little laugh at the memory)* . . . and once I nearly had it! . . . while I was chasing it, it was as if something inside me, something that had been dead for a long, long time, slowly came back to life again. All sorts of strange feelings began to stir inside me . . . and the next thing I knew I was laughing! Can you believe that, Praskovya? Me laughing! In here!

PRASKOVYA: I wish I'd been here for that.

PAVEL: I called you.

PRASKOVYA: I remember that laugh very well. Such a good one it was! But how do we end up with a dead pig?

PAVEL: I'm coming to that. Don't interrupt me.

PRASKOVYA: I'm sorry.

PAVEL: The little butterfly . . .

PRASKOVYA: Yes.

PAVEL: I was chasing it and laughing . . . the way I used to when I was a little boy. A moment of magic, Praskovya! . . . as if it had found . . . in here! . . . a mysterious path back to my childhood . . . back to the meadows where I used to romp and play, with flowers and birdsong all around me, a blue wind-swept sky overhead . . .

PRASKOVYA: That is very beautiful, Pavel.

PAVEL: Oh, yes. So there we were: the butterfly and the little boy . . . Beauty and Innocence! *(Pause)* It settled in that pen.

PRASKOVYA *(At last she understands)*: Oh dear dear dear . . .

PAVEL *(Nodding)*: Beauty and Innocence were joined by the Beast. *(For a few seconds his emotions again leave him at a loss for words)* It was horrible, Praskovya. I saw it coming but there was nothing I could do to stop it. First the mean black little eyes focused, the bristles on its snout started quivering in anticipation . . . but before I could move a muscle it had opened its loathsome mouth and that was the end of it.

PRASKOVYA: Don't take it too much to heart, Pavel. You tried your best, and God will bless you for your efforts.

PAVEL: God will do nothing of the sort. God doesn't give a damn about what goes on in here.

PRASKOVYA *(Not sure she has heard correctly)*: Pavel?

PAVEL: And if he does, there is nothing he can do about it.

PRASKOVYA *(Deeply shocked)*: What are you saying, Pavel Ivanovich!

PAVEL: I'm saying that God has no jurisdiction in here. And do you know why? Because this is Hell! Yes! I know where I am now. I at last know this place for what it really is. Hell! The realm of the damned. *This* is my punishment, Praskovya . . . to watch brutes devour Beauty and then fart . . . to watch them gobble down Innocence and turn it into shit . . . *(Breaking down once again)* And it is more than I can endure. I'm reaching the end, Praskovya. Those few seconds of innocent laughter might well have been the death rattle of my soul.

PRASKOVYA: Come now, Pavel, I know you are very upset but don't exaggerate. You can't have it both ways.

PAVEL: What do you mean?

PRASKOVYA: You can't be both dying *and* in Hell.

PAVEL: Why not?

PRASKOVYA: Because any little child will tell you that Hell is where you will go *after* you're dead.

PAVEL *(Nearly speechless with outrage)*: You are going to split hairs with me at a time like this?

PRASKOVYA: Just thought you might be interested in the truth, Pavel.

PAVEL: Well, I'm not! Because what you call "The Truth" invariably involves the reduction of profound philosophic and moral issues to the level of your domestic triviality.

PRASKOVYA: All right, all right, have it your own way. But at the risk of making you even more angry, Pavel, I think I should also point out that only last week I had to let out your trouser seams because you're putting on a little weight around the waist . . . and now you've just killed a full-grown pig with your bare hands. That doesn't sound like a dying man to me.

PAVEL: I meant it *spiritually*! *Inside!* Didn't you hear me? I was talking about my *soul*.

PRASKOVYA: Oh, I see . . .

PAVEL: No, you don't! You see nothing. The full tragic significance of what is happening in here is beyond your comprehension. *(To the wall, with its tally of dead flies)* Look! Look at what I've become! Look at what my life has been reduced to. Nine thousand seven hundred and eighty-five dead flies! The days of my one and only life on this earth are passing, while I sit in mindless imbecility at that table swatting flies. And when I get bored with that, what is my other soul-uplifting diversion? Tormenting the pigs. *They* are now a higher form of life than me. That's the truth! They have at least got a purpose. Crude as it may be, pork sausages and bacon does give their lives a meaning . . . which is more than can be said of mine. I'm not deluding myself, am I, Praskovya? I wasn't always like this. The man you married . . . he was like other men, wasn't he? . . . decent and hard-working with dreams and plans for a good and useful life. Remember our last night together before I went off to the war . . . how we sat up in bed and talked about the future and what we were going to do when I came back . . . the plans we had for a family, for more pigs and a bigger and better sty. That was *Me* . . . the same man whose greatest pleasure now is to flatten another fly on the table top. Do you know what his ambition is? A hundred thousand squashed flies. *(Wandering around the sty)* And to think that my greatest fear was that I would lose my mind. *(Hollow laughter)* That would have been a happy ending compared to what is really in store for me in here. The punishment reserved for me, Praskovya, is to live on in total sobriety and sanity knowing that I am losing my soul, that a day will come when I'll be no better than the brute I killed. And when that has happened, should Beauty chance to cross my path again . . . *(He swats the imaginary butterfly as he did the flies)* And look at what I'll be using! *(The tattered slipper)* Do you recognize this? Can you detect any trace of its former delicacy and beauty under the crust of filth that now covers it? My mother's slippers! There were my most cherished possessions. Look at them now. *(Hurls his slippers into one of the pens)* There . . . let's make a thorough job of it . . . turn them into shit as well. A life with nothing sacred left in it is a soulless existence, Praskovya. It is not a life worth living.

Praskovya does not know how to respond. She alternately nods and then shakes her head and in this fashion gets through a respectful silence before again venturing to speak.

PRASKOVYA *(Timidly)*: Pavel . . . I don't mean to interrupt but . . . can I ask a question? *(No response from Pavel)* What immediate effect does all of that have on things . . . and the situation in here. . . . What I mean is . . . I don't want to interfere but it is getting on for suppertime and well . . . must I go on with it . . . or what? *(No response from Pavel)* I was making cabbage soup and dumplings. *(No response)* Pavel?

PAVEL *(Violently)*: I heard you!

Another pause.

PRASKOVYA: Well?

PAVEL *(It is not easy for him)*: Have we got a little cinnamon for the dumplings?

PRASKOVYA: Yes.

PAVEL: Soup and dumplings.

SCENE 3

The Midnight Walk

The pigsty. A lot more time has passed. There is yet another layer of graffiti on the walls, consisting this time of obscenities and rude drawings of the pigs. The animals are in a subdued mood as the scene starts. It is night. A lit candle on the table. Pavel is on his bunk, propped up against pillows. He appears to be a very sick man. Labored, desperate breathing. Praskovya is in attendance. Laid out in readiness is a woman's outfit: dress, shawl, hat and shoes.

PAVEL *(Struggling to speak)*: Is it time yet?

PRASKOVYA: Just a little longer.

PAVEL: You said that at least an hour ago.

PRASKOVYA: There are still a few lights on in the street. It won't be safe until they are all out. Be patient.

PAVEL: "Be patient"! I'm dying . . . of suffocation . . . and she says, "Be patient"!

PRASKOVYA: Shall I keep fanning you?

PAVEL: Useless! All that does . . . is circulate . . . the stench . . . and foul air in here. I need fresh air . . . fresh air . . . fresh air . . .

PRASKOVYA: And you are going to get it. Just hang on a few minutes more. It won't be long now before the village will be in bed and fast asleep and then we can take our chance . . . *(Makes the sign of the cross)* And may God help us. Let me say once again, Pavel, that I'm feeling more than just a little nervous. You've had some strange ideas in here, but this one. . . . If it wasn't for your condition I would never have agreed to it. So remember your promise . . . no arguments when we get out there. You don't know your way around anymore so *I'm* leading the way, and we're going as far as the big poplar and then coming back. If you are up to it and it looks safe, we can maybe think about a more roundabout route for our return. But that's all. Agreed?

She sees that Pavel is crying.

Now what's the matter? Really, Pavel, you spend half your time in tears these days.

PAVEL: Give me your hand . . . feel my heart.

PRASKOVYA: Oh my word yes! What's that all about, Pavel?

PAVEL: Fear. I'm frightened.

PRASKOVYA: Then shouldn't we abandon this crazy idea?

PAVEL: No . . . no . . . it's not just *that*. Everything! My whole life. For all of his fifty-one years, Pavel Ivanovich Navrotsky has been a frightened man . . . and I'm so tired of it now, Praskovya . . . tired . . . tired . . .

PRASKOVYA: Don't aggravate your condition with morbid thoughts. Try to look on the bright side of things.

PAVEL: No, I *must* speak. There are things about me that I've kept hidden, unconfessed truths, that choke me tonight as much as the fetid air in here.

PRASKOVYA: All right, Pavel. *I'm* listening.

PAVEL *(Sitting up)*: I'm a coward, Praskovya! Please, no denials . . . I've got to say it. Pavel Ivanovich Navrotsky is a coward. It's true, Praskovya. Where other men are motivated by patriotism, or ambition . . . I have been driven by fear. The other night, knowing that my end is now near, I tried to remember my childhood, tried to recall for the last time just a few images of those carefree, happy years of innocence . . . but do you know what were the only memories that came to me? Frightened little Pavel hiding away from trouble! From big bullies looking for a fight, or my angry father with his belt in his hand . . . hiding away under my bed, in the cupboard under the stairs, in the cellar, in the shed at the bottom of the garden.

I had a secret little book in which I kept a list of all the places I had found to hide. I believed that if I could find a hundred small, dark little places into which I could crawl and lie very still and where no one would find me, then I would be safe all my life. I only got as far as sixty-seven. And it didn't end in my childhood, Praskovya. As I grew up I refined the art of hiding away. I ended up being able to do it even when I was in the middle of a crowd of people! Like our wedding. I've got a terrible confession to make, Praskovya, you married my black suit. I was hiding away inside it at the time. Or that "brave" soldier who waved goodbye to you when he marched off to the war. The only brave thing about him was his uniform. I was hiding away inside that one as well. My courage lasted for as long as those buttons were bright. And how does it all end? In a pigsty! And guess what Pavel Navrotsky is doing in the pigsty? This is number sixty-eight. *(He collapses back on his pillows)*

PRASKOVYA: There, you've got it off your chest. Do you feel better now?

PAVEL: No . . . if anything I feel worse. If I don't breathe fresh air within the next few minutes, you'll be hiding me away in my grave before the night is out.

PRASKOVYA: Come now, Pavel . . . none of that! I'll go and check again. *(She exits and returns after a few seconds)* Yes, we can chance it now. All the lights are out.

Pavel, helped by Praskovya, gets to his feet and then struggles into the woman's outfit. A difficult operation because of his condition. At the end of it he is very exhausted and has to support himself by leaning on the table.

PAVEL: Mirror.
PRASKOVYA: What?
PAVEL: Mirror!!

Praskovya fetches a mirror and holds it up so that Pavel can see himself. He straightens up and studies his reflection.

(Tapping a spot on his chest) Have you . . . have you got . . . a little brooch or something. . . ?

Praskovya exits. Pavel adjusts his outfit while she is gone. She returns with a pretty little box covered with seashells in which she keeps her precious things. Pavel rummages through its contents and chooses a brooch. Praskovya pins it on the dress.

PRASKOVYA: Very good!

PAVEL: Not too loose around the waist?

PRASKOVYA: No. In fact, I think that dress looks better on you than it ever did on me.

PAVEL: Really?

PRASKOVYA: Oh, yes. If it wasn't for your whiskers, I'd believe that you were the mother or wife of some good family. Just keep your face covered and say nothing and nobody will be any the wiser. But don't get carried away. If we do meet somebody out there or get stopped or whatever, *I'll* do the talking. The story is that you are my cousin, Dunyasha, from Yakutsk, and she's as deaf as a doornail, "So don't waste your breath talking to her. She can't hear a thing." Ready? *(Makes the sign of the cross)* Say a quiet prayer that there are no hooligans prowling around ready to take advantage of two helpless women.

They sneak out into the night. The assault on Pavel's senses is total—a gentle breeze, the smell of the earth, stars in the sky, crickets and the distant barking of a dog. It is more than he can cope with. After a few deep breaths of freedom, he reels giddily.

Mother of God, what's happening? Pavel? Is this a stroke?

Please don't die on me out here?

PAVEL: The air, Praskovya . . . the fresh air . . . it's making me drunk . . . hold me . . . hold me up, I think I'm going to faint . . .

PRASKOVYA: That settles it! Back into the sty! Come, Pavel, while you're still on your legs. The whole idea is madness. I should never have agreed to it.

PAVEL: No no no . . . it's passing . . . I'll be all right. *(A low soft moan of ecstasy escapes from his lips)*

PRASKOVYA: Not so loud!

PAVEL: Stars, Praskovya . . . stars. . . . Look!

PRASKOVYA: Yes, I can see them! But for God's sake keep your voice down. At this rate we'll have the whole village awake before we've even started.

PAVEL: And the little crickets! Listen! This is not a dream, is it, Praskovya?

PRASKOVYA: No, it isn't, but God knows I wish it was.

PAVEL: Just another dream to torment me when I wake up and find myself back in that shithouse. Pinch me, Praskovya. Come on, pinch me.

She does so.

Ouch! Oh yes, I felt that! So then it's true. I'm awake and all of this beauty, this soul-ravishing beauty is real! Mother Earth . . . I give myself to you.

Opening his arms as if to embrace all of creation, he lurches off into the night. Praskovya follows frantically.

PRASKOVYA: You're going the wrong way! Left . . . Pavel . . . Dunyasha . . . turn left . . .

Pavel arrives at the big poplar. A few seconds later he is joined

*by Praskovya, exhausted and breathless from trying to keep up
with him.*

In heaven's name stop, Pavel! What's the matter with you?
Do you want us to be caught? We're supposed to look like
two sober and sensible women out for a stroll and a breath
of fresh air before bed. You've been tearing through the
night as if a man was after you. We're lucky nobody came
dashing out to defend our virtue. *(Looking around)* Well,
anyway, here we are. Let's rest a few minutes and get our
breath, and enjoy ourselves, then we can make our way
back. But for the sake of my poor old legs, let's take it easy
this time.

Pavel is sniffing the air like a hungry dog.

Yes, wild roses! They've put on quite a show this year.
Masses of them everywhere!
PAVEL *(Still delirious with freedom)*: This is wicked.
PRASKOVYA: What have you done now?
PAVEL: This star-studded, rose-scented magnificence! I have no
moral right to it, Praskovya. My sins have made me an
outcast on this earth, like Adam thrown out of
Eden . . . but here I am trying to sneak back past the
Guardian Angel for one last little taste of Paradise.
PRASKOVYA: Don't worry about it too much. It looks as if the
Almighty had decided to turn a blind eye on what we're up
to otherwise we would have been struck down long ago.
And it's not as if we're going to make a habit of it . . . I
hope.
PAVEL: You know, Praskovya, I thought that in that sty I had
become some sort of moral degenerate, that my soul had
rotted away in the ocean of pig shit and piss I've been
swimming in since God alone knows when. But that is not

true! I still have it!

PRASKOVYA: Moderate your language, Pavel. That is not the way a good woman talks.

PAVEL: Oh, most definitely . . . I feel it tonight . . . I feel it stirring!

PRASKOVYA: All right, I believe you. But now that you know you've still got it, don't let it stir you up too much. You're making me nervous, Pasha.

PAVEL: I can't help myself. That little breeze wafting the scent of roses this way is at work on my emotions as if it were a hurricane. I am aroused! I have urges!

PRASKOVYA: God help us. I saw it coming.

PAVEL: Strange and powerful urges!

PRASKOVYA: Urges to do what, Pavel?

PAVEL: That road! That road stretching before us, Praskovya . . . it beckons!

PRASKOVYA *(Firmly)*: No.

PAVEL: Yes! Let's keep walking.

PRASKOVYA *(Even more firmly)*: And I say no! This is as far as we go. We haven't got enough time left, Pavel, 'specially if we're going to take it easy going back. These summer nights are very short. It won't be long now before the sparrows start chirping and we see a little light in the east.

PAVEL: No no no no . . . you don't understand. I'm not talking about adding just a few miserable minutes to this stolen little outing. I'm saying: Let's follow that road into the Future!

PRASKOVYA: To where? It leads to Barabinsk, Pavel.

PAVEL: All right! So it's to Barabinsk we go . . . and then beyond! The Future, Praskovya. A New Life.

PRASKOVYA: What are you suggesting, Pavel?

PAVEL: Escape.

PRASKOVYA: You mean. . . ?

PAVEL: Yes, that's right . . . the unmentionable . . . the

unthinkable . . . Escape! What's the matter with you, Praskovya! Have you been so brainwashed that you've forgotten what the word means?

PRASKOVYA: But what about the house, Pavel . . . all our things . . . the pigs. . . ?

PAVEL: Turn our back on the lot and walk away. Yes! Abandon everything. There must be no going back. If we go back, we'll never do it.

PRASKOVYA: So we must set off, just as we are.

PAVEL: Yes. Here and now!

PRASKOVYA: You dressed as a woman, not a ruble in our pockets. . . !

PAVEL: We'll live like gypsies.

PRASKOVYA: You don't know anything about gypsies, Pavel! You've gone mad tonight. I'm not listening to you anymore.

PAVEL: If I have, it's a divine madness because it has given me a vision of my Freedom. Yes, Praskovya! I'd rather die in a ditch beside that road, under the stars with a clean wind in my hair, than return to that sty and die of suffocation from pig fart.

PRASKOVYA: Pavel, please calm down and listen to me. If you take to that road and go on walking, you won't die in a ditch with the stars and the wind and all the rest of it. You'll end up in jail or in front of a firing squad. Come to your senses, Pavel! Look at you. You'll never get away with it in broad daylight. Your splendid "future" will last as long as it takes to walk to the next village where the police will nab you. Come now, Pasha . . . we're too old for all these grand ideas. Let's just turn around quietly and go home.

PAVEL: Home? Don't use that word! I don't know what it means any more. Waiting for me back there is a foul dungeon which I share with a dozen other uncouth inmates. No . . . no . . . no . . . I've got this far . . . I'm not going back.

PRASKOVYA *(Giving up)*: Okay, Pavel, I've tried my best. If that's the way you want it, go ahead, take to the road and walk. Believe me I will pray very hard that you find your "freedom" and enjoy a long and happy "future."

PAVEL: What do you mean? Aren't you coming?

PRASKOVYA: No, you walk alone. I've had enough. This is as far as I go.

PAVEL: You can't just abandon me, Praskovya.

PRASKOVYA: You've got it the wrong way around, Pavel. *You* are abandoning *me. You're* the one who is leaving. What are you waiting for?

PAVEL: You seem to be in a hurry to get rid of me, Praskovya.

PRASKOVYA: It's just that I want to get home while it's still dark, but I also feel I should at least wave goodbye to you when you set off.

PAVEL: All right, all right . . . I'm going. *(Adjusting his dress)* So then, this is it. Goodbye, Praskovya.

PRASKOVYA: Goodbye, Pavel.

Pavel takes a few uncertain steps along the road. Praskovya waves. Pavel stops and then returns to her side.

PAVEL: Tell you what . . . I'll strike a bargain. If you wait here with me for the sunrise, I'll go back with you. Please, Praskovya! Do you realize how long it has been since I last felt the golden light of a new day . . . saw my shadow on the earth! That's all I ask. It can't be long now surely. Look . . . isn't the sky already turning gray over there?

PRASKOVYA: If it is, then it also won't be long before we find ourselves in very serious trouble. By the time the sun rises half the village is already up and about the day's business. No, Pavel. This is the end of it. It's not that I don't love you, but my nerves can't take any more. After they've arrested you, tell them they'll find me at home. *(She abandons Pavel at the big poplar and scuttles off back home)*

PAVEL: Are you leaving me?

PRASKOVYA *(A voice in the night)*: Yes.

PAVEL: You can't!

PRASKOVYA: I have!

Pavel, irresolutely, tries to stand his ground. As the first light of day waxes, his courage wanes. Eventually . . .

PAVEL: Praskovya! *(He hurries after Praskovya)*

The sty. Praskovya is waiting. Pavel bursts in—a dishevelled, desperate figure. He has been running, and it takes him a few seconds to get his breath back.

PAVEL: Your pious soul will rejoice to hear that an Avenging Angel of the Lord did appear to chase Adam out of Eden. It took the form of a big, vicious brute with a black muzzle and long white fangs who came snarling at me out of the darkness. I've got his teeth marks on my ankle to prove it. *(Looking around with disbelief)* I don't believe it! I'm back in here. I was actually out in the world . . . the world of men and women, trees and flowers, of sunsets and sunrises . . . it was there in front of me, a road leading to a new life, but of my own free will, I turned around and came *running* . . . yes, *running*! . . . back to this. Oh, God. I was so near escaping. One small burst of courage! That was all it needed. And if you had given me a little support and encouragement, Praskovya, I would have found that courage. A few words would have done it. "Here's my hand, Pavel. Let's walk." So what if it had only lasted a few golden hours? Wouldn't that have been better than the next eternity of this? But no, here I am again. . . . And why? Because you have finally come to believe that this is where I

belong. My Home! Yes, that wasn't just an insensitive slip
of the tongue out there, was it!! That *is* what you believe!

Praskovya tries to say something.

So what does that make me? A pig?

Another attempt from Praskovya to speak.

Some sort of superior pig that God has endowed with
language and rational thought? Your favorite, your pet pig
who you favor with bowls of cabbage soup and dumplings
while the others get hogwash. Is that how you see me now?
    *(He leaves Praskovya, wanders around the sty and then
steadies himself for a final declaration)* For thirty years I have
tried to hang on to my manhood in here, tried to defend
my dignity against assaults on every front . . . body, mind
and soul. Your betrayal is the last straw. I am broken. These
are the last words that you will ever hear from me. I
abandon my humanity! From now on, Praskovya, feed me
at the trough with the others.

*He tears off his clothes and throws himself naked into one of
the pens with the pigs. A few seconds of silence while Praskovya
considers this development. She then gets up and goes over to
the pen where Pavel has joined the pigs.*

PRASKOVYA: I hope you're not being serious, Pavel. *(No response)*
Because if you are . . . well . . . I think you might have
gone too far this time. This is very insulting, I'll have you
know, both to me and to God. I married a man, not a pig,
and as far as the Almighty is concerned, I'm sure he'd like
me to remind you that you're supposed to be made in His
image. So for the sake of everybody concerned, please get
out of there. *(No response)*

You are provoking me, Pavel. I warn you I might do something we are both going to regret. So for the last time, I beg you. Get out of there.

(She kneels and prays) Dear Lord Jesus Christ, I know it's all wrong to be down on my knees praying to you in a pigsty, but I need your understanding and forgiveness at this moment as never before in my life. Dear Lord Jesus, I am being tempted to sin very badly. Feelings I never knew I had have got hold of my soul and are trying to make me do wicked, wicked things. The reason for this urgent prayer, Lord Jesus, is to beg you, to beseech you . . . please *don't* give me the strength to resist temptation. Amen.

(She gets up and fetches Pavel's stick. She rolls up her sleeves, kicks off her shoes, tucks her shirt into her bloomers and then climbs into the pen) This is going to hurt me every bit as much as I intend hurting you.

Pavel gets his first whack. A cry of pain.

Out you get! Come on. Move!

Another whack, another cry. Pavel crawls frantically out of the sty. Praskovya keeps after him.

If you want me to stop . . . *ask* me.

Another blow . . . another cry.

You better speak to me, Pavel, because I hate to say it, but this isn't hurting me at all.

PAVEL *(Can't take any more)*: Stop! Stop! You're killing me!
PRASKOVYA: Don't worry, I won't go that far. But I would like to hear a few more words.

Another whack.

PAVEL: Stop it, Praskovya! Have you gone mad?
PRASKOVYA: Now onto your legs.
PAVEL: No. Leave me alone.

Praskovya puts all she's got into one final blow.

All right! All right! *(He crawls to his feet)*
PRASKOVYA: We've done it!
PAVEL: Help me, Praskovya . . . help me!

Praskovya fetches a bucket of water and empties it over him.

PRASKOVYA: You're on your two legs again, Pavel, and talking. That's as much as I can do for you. Now help yourself . . .

She exits. Pavel alone—naked, covered in mud and hurting—a picture of abject misery.

SCENE 4

Orders from the Commissar

Night. Pavel, still naked and dirty, but now wrapped in one of his blankets. He sits, a lonely, desolate figure in the Stygian gloom of the sty. He is totally exhausted and talking to himself in a desperate effort to stay awake. Pig noises as usual from the darkness.

PAVEL: Right step, march, left step, march. Comrade Private, head up . . . come on. . . . Up! Up! Open your eyes.
   (Responding) There.
   Wide open!
   They are.

No, they're not. You're falling asleep again.

Because I am tired for God's sake! I am utterly and totally exhausted.

No no no no, Pavel. If you close your eyes and sleep through another night in here, that will be the end of it.

Then do something. Help me!

I'll tell you a story, Pavel. Are you listening? Once upon a time, in a small village, there was a very very stupid man who woke up one morning and decided that he wanted to be a pig.

Oh shut up!

Don't you want to hear the rest of it? It's got a very funny ending, Pavel. His feet turned into trotters, his nose becomes a snout . . .

I said shut up! *(Looking around)* I'm awake. Thank God. That was close! Okay . . . back to work. Where were we? Yes . . . we were dealing with the extremely critical situation which has developed in here, and we were . . . going to . . . we were going . . . to . . . we . . . were . . . going . . . to . . . *(His head falls forward. A few seconds of sleep)*

PAVEL!!!

(He snaps awake with terror and guilt) I didn't do it! I didn't do it! I swear I didn't do it!

(An oily, evil voice) Naughty . . . naughty! You got away with a few seconds there, didn't you? Very naughty, little Pavel. I think Daddy should take off his belt and drag you out from under the bed and give you a bloody good thrashing!!

(Abject terror) I'm sorry, I'm sorry. I won't do it again.

Don't waste our time with promises. We've had them from you before and they've all come to nothing. You know something, Navrotsky . . . you're a total failure . . . and a pathetic one at that! Praskovya was right . . . all you've learned in here is how to whine and wallow in self-pity.

(Nodding encouragement) Good, good . . . keep it up keep it up . . .

Oh, you're finally interested in the truth, are you! Right! You are also a cowardly deserter . . . a traitor to your Motherland. . . . And for what? Can you even remember why you betrayed your country and its people? A pair of slippers. *(Heavily sarcastic tone of voice)* A pair of pretty red slippers which dear old Mama made for her darling little Pavel.

DON'T drag my mother into this! Say anything you like about me but *leave my mother alone*!

What do you mean "leave her alone"! Giving birth to you makes the old bitch an accomplice in all your treachery.

STOP NOW!

(Pause)

WELL done, Pavel. Well done. Brutal and ugly . . . but it worked. Head clear? Oh yes. Crystal clear. Then back to work. No sleep in here until we have found a solution to my now very desperate dilemma. To do that we first need to get to the Root of the Matter, the Root of the Problem. And while we're digging around looking for it, let's keep an eye open at the same time for the Last Straw so that at long last we can get on with it and break the bloody Camel's Back. But hang on now, not so fast! Why waste a perfectly good last straw on imaginary camels when we've got so many fucking real pigs that need to have their backs broken? Now we're getting somewhere. We are going to take that Last Straw and break the back of every fucking pig in here. *(Wild laughter)* Crack crack crack crack crack crack crack. Bravo! You've done it, Pavel . . . Pavel . . . Pavel . . . Pavel . . . *(His lunacy spirals away into a voice of quiet and final despair)* Pavel . . . Pavel . . . stop now. Leave

the pigs alone. And if you can't do that . . . why don't you
then just let them go?

(Pause. Pavel floats back slowly out of his delirium) Who
said that? Where did that thought come from?

Me.

(To his mirror) You said that?

Yes.

Say it again.

Those animals have endured enough abuse from you,
Pavel. Why don't you just let them go now?

Just like that? Just . . .

That's right. Just open the doors, then open the pens
and let them go.

*(Pavel is left almost speechless by the unexpectedness of the
idea)* Unbelievable! So simple . . . so obvious! . . . just let
them go. Yes yes yes . . . of course! It makes total sense.
Just . . . open the doors, open the pens and let them go!

(Back to his mirror) Then do it, Pavel.

Now?

Yes. Now! What are you waiting for?

All right, all right. Hold your horses while I think about
my pigs. Your suggestion might be simple, but that doesn't
mean it's easy. It involves me ending a relationship that has
survived decades of filth and nonsense and mutual abuse. I
can't just turn my back on it and walk away as if it meant
nothing.

(Laughing at himself in disbelief) My God, Pavel, you're
amazing! You're up to your old tricks, aren't you? You're
stalling for time. Yes, we've caught you at it again . . .
backing away from the moment of decision and action.
Well, it has got to stop! You are going to do it and you are
going to do it now. Open the doors, open the pens and let
them go. That's an order.

All right. All right. *(A terrified Pavel obeys orders. His first move is to throw open the doors to the outside world. He then goes around the pens, waking up the pigs)* Wake up! Wake up! *(Kicking and rattling boards)* Come on! It's all over. Your hour of liberation has come. The Commissar has ordered your immediate and unconditional release.

Pig noises increase in volume and agitation as the animals stir into life.

All of you . . . onto your trotters. . . . Can't you smell it? Freedom! Now out . . . out . . . out . . .

Pavel opens the pens. The pandemonium rises to a powerful climax as the animals stampede out of the sty. Praskovya appears. Nightgown and lamp. She sees the open door, the empty pens and realizes what Pavel has done. The sound of liberated, squealing pigs recedes in the distance. A few stunned seconds as the two of them listen to the virginal silence in the sty. Praskovya sits down next to Pavel.

PRASKOVYA *(Whisper)*: It's like being in church, isn't it? You feel you've got to say everything in a whisper . . . and think only good thoughts. And so . . . suddenly so calm. And peaceful. My word, Pavel, this is very hard to believe, you know. I never thought it could ever feel like this in here. All the years and years of shouting and violence . . . just gone! *(Shaking her head)* No. This has got to be a dream.

PAVEL: You're awake, Praskovya.

PRASKOVYA: It's really all over?

PAVEL: Yes.

PRASKOVYA: How did you do it?

PAVEL: I obeyed orders.

PRASKOVYA: What do you mean? Orders from who?

PAVEL *(Pointing to the mirror)*: Him. "The Commissar!" Don't

ask me where he came from or what he was doing in here.
A good soldier, which I never was, doesn't ask questions.
He just obeys orders. They were very simple. "Open the
doors, open the pens and let them go."

PRASKOVYA: Just like that.

PAVEL: Just like that.

PRASKOVYA *(Suppressed laugh but still whispering)*: I think
there's something wrong with me. You've just chased our
livelihood out into the night . . . our only source of income
. . . our one and only security . . . we sit here on the brink
of ruin and all I want to do is laugh. What about you?

PAVEL: I feel nothing.

PRASKOVYA: Well, I'm sorry, but I can't help it . . . I want to
laugh.

PAVEL: Go ahead.

PRASKOVYA: You don't laugh in church, Pavel!

*But she does so all the same. Praskovya has a long, side-
splitting silent laugh at themselves and their ruination . . .
gestures to the open doors, the empty pens, themselves . . . "All is
kaput" . . . etc., etc. Her laugh is infectious. Exhausted as he is,
Pavel manages a faint flicker of a response.*

And now I want to cry.

PAVEL: Go ahead. You're allowed to do that in church, aren't
you?

PRASKOVYA: Oh, yes . . . and as loud as you like. *(Wiping her
eyes)* Oh, Pavel, I'm so proud of you! I would never have
had the imagination or the courage to do it.

PAVEL: Imagination? Courage? Who are you talking about,
Praskovya?

PRASKOVYA: You.

PAVEL *(Shaking his head)*: It wasn't like that at all. It was
exhaustion that did it. Total and final mental, physical and

spiritual exhaustion. I *had* to do something, and that was all I could think of.

PRASKOVYA: This is no time for modesty, Pavel. With that one bold move you have freed us. Let me confess to you now that I had finally given up all hope of us ever escaping from it. I had come to believe that only death would end our misery . . . and I was more than ready for mine. In fact, if you're interested in the truth, Pavel, I was down on my knees telling the Good Lord as much when I heard the commotion down here. But instead, here we sit like two ordinary people with nothing better to do. I don't know about you, but I feel a little light-headed and silly . . . silly enough in fact to want to sing a little song . . .

PAVEL: A song! That's right! People . . . sing, don't they?

PRASKOVYA: When they're happy, but sometimes also when they're sad. Mine would have been a happy song.

PAVEL: Do you still know one?

PRASKOVYA: I think so. *(She sings a little happy song)*
So what is the next bold move, Pavel?

PAVEL *(The open doors)*: Isn't it obvious?

PRASKOVYA: You're going out there again?

PAVEL *(Nods)*: But I won't hid away in your dress this time. I'm going out there as myself. *(A helpless gesture)* I didn't know it was coming. I thought I was just getting rid of the pigs so that I could have a little peace and quiet in here. I wanted to close my eyes and sleep more than I've wanted anything in my whole life. But when they started stampeding through those doors to their freedom. . . !!! God, Praskovya, it was epic! The stuff of history. I wanted to join them. If I'd had any clothes on I would have led that charge of liberation out into the world.

PRASKOVYA: You are going to surrender to the authorities?

PAVEL: Yes. It's a crooked fate that ties up a man's freedom and his surrender in the same bundle, but I've got no choice.

(The weak and desperate little smile of the faint-hearted) I
think it's another order . . . to go out there and face
judgment and take my punishment. It's been a long
loneliness in here. I've forgotten what it means, what it
feels like to look into another man's eyes . . . or to be
looked at by them. I'm still frightened . . . but there is
something else now as well and it's bigger than my
fear . . . I'm homesick, Praskovya, for other men and
women. I don't belong in here. Even if my punishment
turns out to be a firing squad . . . those men, looking at me
down the barrels of their guns, will be "home" in a way this
sty could never have been.

PRASKOVYA: So then let's do it. I'll get you something to wear.
(Starts to leave and then stops) It's a pity we can't take on
that walk to Barabinsk. I'm ready for it now.

*She exits. First faint light of the new day through the open
doors. Pavel gets a bucket of water and starts to wash himself.
The graffiti on the walls catches his attention. He takes a rag
and tries to clean it off, too exhausted to do a thorough job.
Praskovya comes back with Pavel's black wedding suit. She has
changed out of her nightgown.*

PAVEL: What do you have there?
PRASKOVYA: Don't you recognize it? Your wedding suit.
PAVEL: My God. That goes back a few years. Is it still wearable?
PRASKOVYA: Oh, yes. After all that drama we had about your
uniform, I've made a point of looking after this very
carefully. I had a feeling you might need it again one day.

Pavel starts to change into the suit.

How are we going to do it, Pavel? There aren't any
anniversary celebrations on the go this time. I don't think it

will work to just stand on a street corner and announce to the world who you are and what you've done. I'm not sure anybody will bother to listen to you. There are all sorts of loonies around these days and nobody pays them any attention except the police. Maybe that's your best idea, the police station.

PAVEL *(Offended)*: I'm not just a common criminal, Praskovya. As I remember it, the *Military Manual* listed desertion as one of the most serious offences a soldier could commit. I'll hand myself over at the military barracks. *(He is now dressed)* Come . . . let's go.

PRASKOVYA: If it's any consolation, I think we're in time for the sunrise you missed yesterday.

They leave the sty.